Amazing Annuals

AMAZING ANNUALS

*More than 300 container and garden plants
for summer-long color*

Marjorie Mason Hogue

FIREFLY BOOKS

A FIREFLY BOOK

Published by Firefly Books Ltd. 1999

First printing

Library of Congress Cataloguing-in-Publication is available.

Canadian Cataloguing-in-Publication Data
Hogue, Marjorie Mason
    Amazing annuals: more than 300 container and garden plants for summer-long color
Includes index.
ISBN 1-55209-307-7
1. Annuals (Plants) – North America.   I. Title.
SB422.H63 1999   635.9'312'097   c98-932617-9

Published in Canada in 1999 by
Firefly Books Ltd.
3680 Victoria Park Avenue
Willowdale, Ontario
Canada M2H 3K1

Published in the United States in 1999 by
Firefly Books (U.S.) Inc.
P.O. Box 1338, Ellicott Station
Buffalo, New York
USA 14205

A DENISE SCHON BOOK

Design: Counterpunch / Linda Gustafson, Peter Ross
Editor: Charis Cotter
Copy Editor: Wendy Thomas
Index: Barbara Schon
Production: Denise Schon Books Inc.

Printed and bound in Canada by Transcontinental

Photo credits: Mason Hogue Gardens pp. 11, 18, 19 top, 20 bottom, 23 top, 31, 38, 44 top, 48, 51, 53, 58, 62 bottom, 79, 81, 94, 100 top, 114, 124, 126, 130, 132, 134, 136, 140; Andrew Leyerle pp. 13, 14, 19 bottom, 20 top, 21, 22, 23 bottom, 24, 26, 29, 30, 32, 35, 36, 41, 42, 44 bottom, 45, 46, 47, 49, 50, 52, 54, 55, 56, 57, 59, 60, 61, 62 top, 66, 67, 68, 69, 71, 72, 73, 74, 80 top, 92 top, 96, 98, 99, 100 bottom, 101, 102 top, 103, 105, 108, 111, 112, 113, 116, 118, 120, 122, 128, 138, 142, 144; Patricia Cook p. 63; Ogelvee p. 65; Norseco pp. 70, 102 bottom; International Flower Bulb Center pp. 76, 77, 78, 82, 83, 84, 85 top, 86, 87, 88, 89, 90, 91, 92 bottom, 93, 97, 104, 106; John Valleau p. 85 bottom.

The Publisher acknowledges the financial support of the Government of Canada through the Book Publishing Industry Development Program for its publishing activities.

This book is dedicated to my grandchildren —
Samantha, Jessica, Stephanie, Matthew, Bradley,
Emily, Derek, and Geneviève.

    May they, too, always know the joy of growing
plants and hopefully they will have pleasant memo-
ries of Grandma's Garden — remembering not only
the admonition to "stay on the paths"!

Acknowledgements

Thank you to my parents and grandparents who
started me growing plants!

To John Patterson who encouraged me to collect
plants and to speak and write about them.

To Jeff, my son and plant collecting partner and
his wife Laura for her patience with us and especially
her computer skills.

To Pat Redwood who grows my plants in her
containers with such enthusiasm and care.

To Denise Schon Books who prodded me
through this endeavour.

To all my family and friends for their interest
and encouragement.

And most especially for my husband Réal who
suffered with me the nine months of agonizing to
get it all down on paper!

Contents

Introduction

Annuals are often dismissed as boring or second-rate. It's true that certain types of impatiens, petunias and marigolds have definitely been overused, but it's not hard to find exciting new annuals to revitalize your plantings. Have you seen the new yellow seashell impatiens? Or the petunias that cascade 3 feet (1 m) from a window box? Or the tiny 'Lemon Gem' marigolds with masses of dime-sized yellow blooms?

Enjoying plants has been a way of life for me since the age of one when I picked all my grandmother's prized double petunias and proudly proclaimed them "Pretty!" My grandmother averted my mother's scolding by telling her that I should never be chastised for loving flowers. My family has been gardening for several generations: I learned to count to 100 with the help of peony buds in my great-grandfather's acre of perennials, which he grew to sell as cut flowers, and I followed my father's footsteps between the rows of vegetables in our market garden.

Much later, after a 13-year career as a teacher, I decided to enter the field of horticulture full time. I worked in a large garden center for 19 years, during which time I amassed a collection of 500 varieties of pelargoniums (tender geraniums). Then it was time, with my son's help and my husband's encouragement, to start our own small specialty plant nursery, Mason Hogue Gardens.

We originally focused on hardy perennials and bulbs, but neither my son Jeff nor I can resist trying a new plant when we see it listed in a catalogue. In the last few years there have been so many introductions of tender plants that it's been almost impossible to try them all — *Alonsoa, Anagallis, Angelonia, Anisodontea, Asarina* — the list goes on and on. When customers visit our display gardens, they are excited by the many unusual plants they see and are frequently surprised when they realize that the ones they like best are annuals!

It really is a shame that some of the best flowers in a gardener's palette are overlooked simply because they're not perennials. Much as we love our perennial beds, it is difficult to have masses of bloom all summer long without incorporating some annuals into the scheme. Many great gardens have annuals drifted through the clumps of perennials. Even the famous double border in the Royal Horticultural Society's garden at Wisley in England uses dahlias, cleome, bidens and cosmos in this way.

This is a book for every type of gardener — the beginner who needs help getting started, the do-it-yourselfer who wants to grow masses of plants from seeds and cuttings, the person who gardens on a small balcony, the creative type who wants a garden different from all the others on the block,

AMONG THE COSMOS

even the armchair gardener who just enjoys reading about plants — but most especially, it's for anyone who has mastered perennials and is now ready to add annuals for the finishing touch.

I have provided detailed descriptions of many different kinds of annuals: annuals grown from cuttings, seeds and bulbs; annuals to grow for their foliage; annuals to climb and trail; and annuals to grow for fragrance. A whole section on container gardening will take you through the exciting process of potscaping, step by step. A chart tells you everything you need to know to cultivate about 180 seed-grown annuals. You can discover how to care for your annual garden and how to reproduce some of your favorite plants in the section on propagation and culture.

To my way of thinking, a truly great garden encompasses all types of plants. Trees and shrubs form the framework and perennials make up the body, but annuals, in the ground and in containers, are the crowning glory.

ABOUT ANNUALS

What is an annual?

Annuals are plants that grow, flower, produce seed and die in one growing season. Like a fireworks display, they are fantastic — but fleeting. Each year I try a host of new annuals. Although some prove incompatible with my garden scheme, I invite many back again and again, and the self-seeders decide for themselves never to leave. Mother Nature usually positions them in the most charming locations, but if these self-invited guests become too numerous, their seedlings make great compost.

Some annuals are described as hardy, which means that the seeds and resulting seedlings are capable of withstanding frost and can be planted directly into the ground in early spring. If started indoors they do not require additional heat to germinate. Sweet peas, sunflowers and nasturtiums are all examples of hardy annuals.

Half-hardy annuals can be planted outdoors after the soil has warmed up, but because this

Argemone grandiflora 'White Prickly Poppy' provides bloom in a sunny, dry garden.

delays bloom until mid- to late summer, they are usually started indoors, 6 to 12 weeks prior to the last frost-free date. They require temperatures of 65° to 75°F (18° to 24°C) to germinate. Marigolds, petunias and snapdragons fall into this category.

Tender annuals shiver at the first hint of cold. They must be started indoors and not placed outside until both the soil and air temperature have warmed up. They need temperatures of 70° to 80°F (21° to 26°C) to germinate. Impatiens, flowering vinca and celosia are tender annuals.

Also treated as annuals are the tender perennials that perform well in their first season, whether grown from seed or cuttings, but they must be sheltered from northern winters if they are to continue living. Examples of tender perennials are geraniums (pelargoniums), coleus and fuchsias.

Biennials

Many people are confused by the term "biennial." Just think of biennials as slow annuals: it takes them two years instead of one to grow, set seed and die. In the first year, they produce a rosette of leaves that lives over the winter; in the second year, they flower, produce seed and die. If you don't let them produce seed (by removing the spent flower stalk at ground level as soon as the blooms are finished) you can often trick them into living on and blooming again the next year.

Don't automatically dismiss biennials as being too much trouble. Simply plant the same variety for two consecutive years. Then you'll always have first-year rosettes and second-year blooming plants. As long as your garden isn't heavily

mulched, they will reseed themselves and sometimes produce unusual combinations.

Some of my favorite biennials suit a cottage-style garden: sweet William (*Dianthus barbatus*), Canterbury bells (*Campanula medium*) and foxgloves (*Digitalis purpurea*). The recently discovered *Angelica gigas* from Korea has dramatic impact: its head of burgundy bloom opens atop 6-to-8-foot (1.8 to 2.4 m) stems in late summer. Two other giants that I wouldn't be without are the silver Scottish thistle (*Onopordum acanthium*) and the stately mullein (*Verbascum bombyciferum*). Both have first year rosettes of silver velvet. And if you enjoy decorating with everlasting flowers, be sure to include the money plant (*Lunaria biennis*).

Evolution of annuals

Each spring millions of packs of small blooming annuals are offered for sale. They have been mass-produced — seeded and transplanted by machine, grown on rolling tables, automatically watered and fertilized, placed on metal carts, forklifted onto transports and delivered to the waiting public who are hungry for blossoms after a long winter. Only plants that perform well under such conditions are mass-produced: impatiens, begonias, petunias, marigolds, the inevitable white alyssum for edging, and a few others. They are usually short — ranging in height from 4 to 18 inches (10 to 45 cm).

If these are the only annuals you know, you probably consider annuals boring. But times are changing — a whole new realm of annuals is waiting to add excitement to your planting schemes. Some of the more unusual introductions are the 8-foot (2.4 m) tall *Impatiens glandulifera*; the firecracker vine (*Manettia luteo-rubra*) with brilliant red and yellow flowers that will climb to a height of 12 feet (3.5 m); and the exotic pineapple flower (*Eucomis bicolor*), a tropical bulb that will grow in a pot on the patio.

Some of the new annuals were discovered during plant searches in South Africa, Australia and Japan; others have been produced through hybridization by plant breeders, but many have already been popular, fallen out of style and are now being revived.

Looking back over the history of annuals, we find that the first flowers were grown more for herbal than ornamental value. *Calendula officianalis* was used in teas and to make soothing skin ointment and burn treatments. In the 16th and 17th centuries, plant collectors traveled around the world, taking hundreds of varieties of plants back to Europe. Lobelia was found in the Cape of Good Hope. Marigolds, cosmos and dahlias were brought from Central and South America in the 1700s.

By the mid-1800s elaborate bedding-out displays were popular in European parks and large estates. Thousands of gardeners labored in glass houses growing the necessary great number of plants, mainly from cuttings. There was an ongoing debate about whether the plantings should be confined to large groupings of one variety or several complementary types should be laid out in geometric patterns. Short plants were used in carpet bedding: floral clocks, coats-of-arms and monograms.

The Victorians' love of the ornate led to the use of tropical foliage plants: palms, agaves, bananas, crotons, cannas and even cannabis! Then in the late 19th century the cottage-style garden grew in popularity.

In the first half of the 20th century, with the advent of better seed-growing techniques and the disruption of two world wars, the emphasis in horticulture changed to herbaceous perennials and annuals that were easily grown from seed.

Now many Victorian favorites are experiencing a revival: double nasturtiums, double lobelia, marguerite daisies, heliotrope, coleus, and fancy-leaf pelargoniums are available again. Many people who winter in the tropics become familiar with local plants — bougainvillea, mandevilla, hibiscus, and banana trees — and use them at home to create a tropical look during our hot summers, overwintering them in solariums.

Suddenly annuals are being written about in every garden magazine. Christopher Lloyd, a well-known garden writer and the owner of Great Dixter, one of the most visited gardens in England, recently removed a traditional rose garden at Great Dixter and installed a garden of cannas, dahlias, banana trees, and *Verbena bonariensis*. Ian Cooke, a respected English horticulturalist, was instrumental in the formation of the international Half-Hardy Plant Society, whose goal is to study and promote tender perennials. Urs Walser, a renowned professor of horticulture in Germany, also uses drifts of annuals in combination with perennials in his garden at Hermanshof.

I hope this book will introduce you to some new favorites and because the annual revival has just begun, each year will bring many new introductions.

Incorporating annuals into your garden

The glory of annuals is that they are temporary. There's no need to agonize over their placement the way we do with perennials. It is just this characteristic that makes them so valuable in many garden scenarios. Consider the following:

You've just moved to a new home that already has gardens, so the first year should be one of observation. Tuck in some of your favorite annuals (cosmos, nicotiana, bachelor's buttons) to enjoy while you assess what needs doing.

Perhaps your new home is a blank canvas but you're not sure what you want and you're short of cash after such a major expenditure. Remove the grass from the area adjacent to the house, work in some peat moss or some other form of humus, and plant readily available annuals of various heights. Fertilize regularly with a liquid 15-30-15 to produce an explosion of blooms to enjoy while you plan your future garden. By taking this approach, you will eliminate many of the mistakes that are made in haste.

It's spring and you've prepared a new bed but realize that the soil needs more improving before you plant expensive perennials. Fill the space with annuals and in the fall rework the soil and plant perennials. Next spring, plant a few annuals in the spaces between the perennials.

You have a basic perennial garden but there isn't as much bloom as you'd like in August. Again, it's annuals to the rescue. Be prepared for the gaping holes left by oriental poppies, lupins, delphiniums, and *Geranium* 'Johnson's Blue' by having some annuals growing in 5-inch (12 cm) pots ready to fill the space with a burst of color.

When your earliest vegetables (radish, spinach, spring onions) are finished, plant the rows with annuals that make good cut flowers for summer and fall bouquets, such as *Ammi majus*, argyranthemums (marguerite daisies), cosmos, larkspur, snapdragons, and zinnias.

If you love experimenting with color, try choosing just the right annual to complement each of your perennials. *Nicotiana langsdorffii*, with lime-green blossoms and blue stamens, makes a perfect backdrop for the blue-flowered *Nepeta siberica* or *Delphinium grandiflorum*. Cool down the hot spots in your garden with annuals of icy blue (*Salvia farinacea* 'Victoria', nigella [love-in-a-mist], tall *Ageratum* 'Blue Horizon') and pristine white (lavatera, cosmos 'Purity' or 'Sonata White,' *Nicotiana sylvestris*, petunias). If someone in your family has impaired vision, add masses of yellow, the most visible color (bidens, Dahlberg daisy, pansies, gloriosa daisies).

Does your pastel perennial garden seem a little passé now that hot colors are all the rage? Add some red, orange and burgundy annuals. (Red: snapdragons, zinnias, amaranthus, salvia; orange: tithonia, *Cosmos sulphureus*, ursinia, nasturtium; burgundy: celosia, coleus, *Ricinus communis* [castor oil plant]).

Plant fragrant annuals (heliotrope, *Nemesia* 'Confetti,' *Matthiola bicornis* [night-scented stock]) around your sitting area. For evening enjoyment include white annuals that shine after dark (*Ipomoea alba, Nicotiana alata*, lavatera, *Nemesia* 'Innocence'). Camouflage the chain-link fence surrounding your castle with annual vines while more permanent solutions are growing.

If your dream is to create a typical English cottage garden, you simply must include annuals. Not the half-dozen overused varieties available at every garden center and corner store, but poppies, larkspur, sweet William, love-in-a-mist and corn cockle.

If you don't have space for a garden or if you are physically unable to work in one, you can still grow annuals in pots, window boxes and hanging baskets.

Each year I can't resist trying new plants as well as growing old favorites. At planting time, there is always the problem of what to put where. I begin by sorting them according to height. Annuals that will surpass 3 feet (1 m) by mid-summer I place in the back of the border among the tall perennials or in a spot where they will screen an objectionable view. Then I select plants that range from 1 to 3 feet (30 to 100 cm) for the middle of the border, where they'll be planted in drifts to act as fillers. Annuals under 12 inches (30 cm) in height are suitable for planting among perennials to create edges for flower borders or to ensure summer color in rock gardens. Following are lists of some of my favourite annuals for specific garden requirements.

THE GARDEN AT HERMANSHOF

Annuals that grow over 3 feet (1 m) tall

Amaranthus
Ammi majus
Artemisia annua (sweet Annie)
Atriplex hortensis (Orach)
Canna
Cleome spinosa (spider flower)
Cosmos bipinnatus
Dahlia
*Digitalis purpurea
Helianthus annuus

Impatiens glandulifera
Leonitis leonurus
Nicotiana sylvestris
*Oenothera biennis
   (evening primrose)
*Onopordum acanthium
   (Scotch thistle)
Ricinus communis
   (castor oil plant)
Salvia uliginosa

Leonitis leonurus

Sphaeralcea hybrida 'Los Brisas'
Tithonia rotundifolia
   (Mexican sunflower)

Annuals that grow 1 to 3 feet (30 to 100 cm) tall

Ageratum 'Blue Horizon'
Agrostemma githago (corn cockle)
Antirrhinum (snapdragon)
Argyranthemum
   (marguerite daisy)
Bidens 'Golden Goddess'
Centaurea (cornflower,
   bachelor's buttons)
Clarkia elegans 'Apple Blossom'
Consolida ambigua (larkspur)
Cosmos bipannatus 'Versailles'
   or 'Sonata'
Cosmos sulphureus

Euphorbia marginata 'Summer
   Icicle'
Kochia scoparia var. trichophylla
   (burning bush)
Lavatera trimestris
Malva sylvestris 'Zebrina'
Nicotiana alata
Nicotiana langsdorffii
Pelargonium – tall scented
   varieties
Perilla frutescens
Salvia farinacea
*Salvia sclarea

Nicotiana langsdorffii WITH
Ipomoea batatas 'BLACKIE'

Salvia viridis (syn. horminum)
Scabiosa atropurpurea
Silene 'Cherry Blossom'
Verbena bonariensis

*BIENNIALS

Annuals that grow up to 1 foot (30 cm) tall

Antirrhinum (snapdragon)
Bacopa 'Snowflake'
Begonia semperflorens
Brachyscome (Swan River daisy)
Browallia
Calceolaria integrifolia
Catharanthus roseus (vinca,
  Madagascar periwinkle)
Convolvulus tricolor
Dianthus
Diascia
Dyssodia tenuiloba
  (Dahlberg daisy)

Felicia amelloides
Gazania
Iberis umbellata (candytuft)
Ipomoea batatus
  (sweet potato vine)
Linaria maroccana
Lobelia erinus
Myosotis sylvatica
  (forget-me-not)
Nierembergia (cupflower)
Nemesia
Petunia
Portulaca

Brachyscome

Senecio cineraria (dusty miller)
Sanvitalia (creeping zinnia)
Tagetes tenuifolia (marigold)
Torenia
Viola (pansies)
Verbena

Drought-tolerant annuals

My garden has some dry areas that call for drought-tolerant plants that can survive with very little water.

Arctotis
Argemone grandiflora
  (prickly poppy)
Coreopsis
Catharanthus rosea (vinca,
  Madagascar periwinkle)
Convolvulus
Dimorphotheca

Dyssodia tenuiloba (Dahlberg
  daisy)
Eschscholzia californica
  (California poppy)
Gaillardia pulchella
Gazania
Helichrysum bracteatum
Limonium sinuatum (statice)
Melampodium paludosum
Mirabilis jalapa (four o'clock)
Papaver rhoeas (Shirley poppy)
Phacelia campanularia
Portulaca

Convolvulus

Salvia coccinea, S. viridis, etc.
Tagetes tenuifolia (marigold)
Verbena hybrids

Annuals for moist boggy conditions

If I had a moist, boggy site or a garden situated where the downspout from an eavestrough delivered periodic drenchings, I would choose annuals from among these:

Canna lilies
Heliotrope
Impatiens glandulifera

Limnanthes douglasii
Lobelia erinus
Lobelia cardinalis
Matthiola incana (stocks)
Mimulus hybrids
Myosotis (forget-me-not)
Nemophila (baby blue eyes)
Thunbergia alata
Torenia

Torenia 'SUMMER WAVE' BLUE

Annuals for a shady spot

To brighten a shady spot, try planting some of the annuals from this list:

Begonia semperflorens and
   B. tuberosa
Browallia
Cheiranthus syn. *Erysimum*
   (wallflower)
Cleome (spider flower)
Consolida ambigua (larkspur)
Coleus
Cynoglossum amabile
   (Chinese forget-me-not)
Digitalis purpurea (foxglove)

Fuchsia hybrids
Impatiens
Lobelia
Lobularia maritima
   (sweet alyssum)
Lunaria annua (honesty)
Mimulus (monkey flower)
Myosotis (forget-me-not)
Nemophila menziesii
Nicotiana
Nigella damascena (love-in-a-mist)
Oenothera biennis
   (evening primrose)
Pelargonium peltatum
   (ivy geranium)

Impatiens 'SEASHELL' YELLOW

Schizanthus x *wisetononsis*
   (poor man's orchid)
Thunbergia alata
Torenia fournieri
Viola

Early blooming annuals

The first annuals to bloom are always much appreciated; they can withstand late frosts and combine well with spring bulbs and perennials, especially in containers. They can be forgiven if they succumb to the hot days of summer.

Antirrhinum (snapdragon)
Calendula (pot marigold)

*Dianthus barbatus
  (sweet William)
Erysimum (wallflower)
Godetia
Gypsophila elegans
  (baby's breath)
Iberis umbellata (candytuft)
Lathyrus odoratus (sweet pea)
Lobularia maritima
  (sweet alyssum)
Myosotis sylvatica (forget-me-not)

Antirrhinum (SNAPDRAGON)

Papaver nudicaule
  (Iceland poppy)
Schizanthus (poor man's orchid)
Viola (pansies)

Self-seeding annuals

My special favorites are annuals I only have to plant once — they continue to return year after year, sometimes in the most un-expected places! The best self-seeding results are in gardens that are mulched with gravel. Areas mulched with shredded cedar have neither weeds nor self-sown seedlings.

Argemone grandiflora
  (prickly poppy)
Borago officinalis (borage)
*Campanula medium
  (Canterbury bells)

Centaurea (cornflower,
  bachelor's buttons)
Clarkia pulchella
Cosmos
*Digitalis purpurea (foxglove)
Eschscholzia californica
  (California poppy)
Euphorbia marginata
Helianthus annuus (sunflower)
Iberis umbellata (candytuft)
Limnanthes douglasii
  (fried eggplant)
Lobularia maritima
  (sweet alyssum)
*Lunaria annua (honesty)
Malva sylvestris 'Zebrina'

Cosmos

Myosotis sylvatica
  (forget-me-not)
Papaver rhoeas (Shirley poppy)
Papaver somniferum
Portulaca
*Salvia sclarea
Salvia viridis (syn. *S. horminum*)
Tropaeolum majus (nasturtium)
Viola

Annuals for cut flowers

I am loath to cut flowers for bouquets from my carefully orchestrated flower borders. A cutting garden is the answer. The following annuals can be included in the vegetable garden or used to camouflage the work area of the garden.

Ammi majus
Antirrhinum (snapdragon)
Calendula officianalis
Callistephus chinensis
  (China aster)
Celosia plumosa

Centaurea (cornflower,
  bachelor's buttons)
Clarkia elegans
Consolida ambigua (larkspur)
Cosmos
Eustoma grandiflorum
Gypsophila elegans
  (baby's breath)
Lathyrus odoratus (sweet pea)
Moluccella laevis (bells of Ireland)
Pansies
Pelargoniums (tender geraniums)
Salvia farinacea
Verbena bonariensis
Zinnia elegans

Verbena bonariensis

Grasses:
Briza maxima (quaking grass)
Hordeum jubatum
  (squirrel tail grass)
Lagurus ovatus (hare's tail grass)
Setaria italica (foxtail millet)

Everlasting Annuals

The bouquets that I enjoy most are of the everlasting type, which are easy to dry and retain their colors vividly. They remind me of my summer garden during the long winter months.

Ammobium alatum
Bracteantha bracteata syn.
  Helichrysum
Celosia cristata

Celosia plumosa
Celosia spicata 'Flamingo
  Feather'
Gomphrena globosa
Gypsophila elegans
  (baby's breath)
Grasses: see previous list
Limonium sinuatum (statice)
Lunaria annua (honesty)
Moluccella laevis
  (bells of Ireland)

Bracteantha bracteata

Nigella damascena
  (love-in-a-mist)
Xeranthemum annuum
  (immortelle)

Color

The best reason for growing annuals is the ease with which I can change my color scheme. Gardening (exterior decorating!) is influenced by trends, much like interior decorating. In the past decade, pastel colors have been popular, but now the trend is to the hot colors: bright yellow, orange, red and burgundy. These colors make your garden a vibrant, exciting place but also make it appear smaller.

If you wish to create a mood of tranquil serenity and make the garden seem larger, choose blues, pinks, mauves and whites. This combination can actually seem to lower the temperature of an area where the sun beats down relentlessly all day. The coolest combination is one of white, green and silver. At twilight blues and purples become less noticeable, whereas white and yellow continue to shine.

Personal preference is an important factor. The first garden I ever designed had only one stipulation: no yellow! For years, yellow was my least favorite color. Gradually I developed an appreciation for soft lemon yellow and the way it blended with blues. After a recent trip to the gardens of Germany, I realized that my garden needs bright yellow. Yellow is the most visible color – even the visually impaired can see it. If you wish to draw attention to an area or divert attention from an eyesore, strategically placed yellow will do the trick.

The best effect comes from planting drifts of annuals rather than plopping individual plants here and there. Repetition of color in a border leads the eye along it. Unify a perennial border of diverse colors by adding annuals of just one color. If you are unsure of color placement, consult a color wheel – opposites complement each other (orange and blue, violet and yellow). Magnificent effects can be achieved by combining shades of the same color: rose pink, ruby red and burgundy; or salmon pink, coral and scarlet. Right now burgundy is my favorite color because it combines well with everything – giving body to pastel plantings and quieting raucous, bold schemes. Here are some color lists to get you started.

Anagallis 'Skylover'

Annuals by color

BLUE ANNUALS

Agapanthus (lily of the Nile)
Ageratum
Anagallis
Angelonia angustifolia
Asperula orientalis
Borago officianalis (borage)
Brachyscome (Swan River daisy)
Browallia
Callistephus chinensis
  (China aster)
Centaurea (cornflower,
  bachelor's buttons)
Cerinthe major 'Purpurescens'
Convolvulus
Felicia amelloides
Gilia capitata
Laurentia axillaris
Lobelia
Lobularia maritima
  (sweet alyssum)
Myosotis sylvatica (forget me not)
Nemophila
Nierembergia
Nigella damascena
  (love-in-a-mist)
Nolana
Pansies
Petunia
Plectranthus zuliensis
Plumbago auriculata
Salvia farinacea, S. patens, etc.
Scaevola (blue fan flower)
Torenia fournieri
Viola hederacea

YELLOW ANNUALS

Antirrhinum (snapdragon)
Argemone mexicana
Bartonia aurea
Bidens
Calceolaria integrifolia
Calendula officinalis
Chrysanthemum coronarium,
  C. multicaule
Dyssodia tenuiloba (Dahlberg daisy)
Gaillardia pulchella 'Yellow Plums'
Helianthus annuus (sunflower)
Mimulus (monkey flower)
Rudbeckia hirta (gloriosa daisy)
Tagetes (marigold)
Thunbergia alata
Zinnia

ORANGE ANNUALS

Arctotis hirsuta (African daisy)
Canna lily
Calendula officianalis
Cosmos sulphureus
Eschscholzia californica
  (California poppy)
Impatiens
Nemesia strumosa
Pelargonium (tender geranium)
Tagetes (marigold)
Tithonia rotundifolia
  (Mexican sunflower)
Tropaeolum majus (nasturtium)
Ursinia anthemoides
Zinnia

GREEN ANNUALS

Moluccella laevis (bells of Ireland)
Nicotiana langsdorffii
Nicotiana alata 'Lime Green'
Zinnia 'Envy'

PURPLE ANNUALS

Calandrinia grandiflora
Callistephus chinensis
  (Chinese aster)
Heliotrope
Pansy
Petunia
Trachelium caeruleum 'Passion
  in Violet'

PINK ANNUALS

Antirrhinum (snapdragon)
Begonia
Cleome
Dianthus
Diascia
Gypsophila muralis 'Garden
  Bride'
Impatiens
Lathyrus odoratus (sweet pea)
Nemesia 'Confetti'
Nicotiana 'Appleblossom'
Petunia
Phlox drummondii
Portulaca
Verbena
Zinnia

Red Annuals

Antirrhinum (snapdragon)
Amaranthus
Begonia semperflorens and
  B. tuberosa
Celosia clarkia speciosa 'Cherry
  Red'
Cuphea ignea
Dahlia
Gaillardia pulchella 'Red Plums'
Impatiens
Papaver rhoeas (Shirley poppy)
Pelargonium (tender geranium)
Zinnia

White Annuals

Ammi majus
Agapanthus (lily of the Nile)
Argemone grandiflora
  (prickly poppy)
Begonia semperflorens and
  B. tuberosa
Catharanthus roseus (vinca,
  Madagascar periwinkle)
Cosmos bipinnatus
Gypsophila elegans
  (baby's breath)
Impatiens
Lavatera trimestris

Lobelia erinus
Lobularia maritima
  (sweet alyssum)
Nicotiana
Petunia
Salvia farinacea

Burgundy Annuals
  (see also Foliage, p. 104)
Amaranthus
Celosia

Annuals provide summer-long color in the garden.

Fragrance in the garden

When you are handed a beautiful flower, what is your first instinct? To raise it to your nose and sniff. Fragrance in a garden is as important as color and design. It comes not only from blooms but also from foliage, twigs and buds. With some plants, you have to get very close to appreciate their perfume, while others can be detected from across the garden. Some blooms are most scented when the sun is hot; others during the dark of night. White flowers are usually more sweetly perfumed than brightly colored ones.

As a general rule, old unimproved varieties have more fragrance than the new hybrids. Nicotiana, that tall rangy plant with delicious night-scented blooms, now has series named Nikki and Domino, available in white, red, pink and even lime green. They are uniformly compact and very floriferous but unfortunately lacking in perfume. I am testing a new variety in my garden this year, *Nicotiana* x *sanderae* 'Heaven Scent', which promises the fragrance of the old-fashioned types with the robust habit of modern hybrids. I hope it proves to be as good as its name!

Fragrance is a very personal thing. What to one person may be exotic to another is overpowering and to yet another non-existent! What's the best way to decide which plants to use to add fragrance to your garden? Start sniffing – in friends' gardens, public gardens and garden centers. Write down the names of those you find most appealing.

Plan carefully for some fragrance in each area of your garden for each season. Place your scented plants so you'll be near them – along walkways, at doorways, near your favorite resting place or beside windows that are usually open.

The following is a sampler of some of the scented plants you may wish to include in your garden. For more suggestions, see the list on page 29.

Sweet alyssum, with its honeyed aroma, will often reseed itself, sometimes in peculiar places rather than the neat border where you originally planted it. The pink and blue varieties are not as sweetly scented as the white. Heliotrope, with its deep purple blooms and dark foliage, contrasts well with other plants. Again, the white variety is more fragrant than the blue. *Matthiola incana* is the highly perfumed stock referred to as sweet gilly flower in romantic novels. The exotic *Datura* is fragrant but also poisonous. No garden would be complete without the sweet faces and scent of pansies. Many people like the pungent foliage of nasturtiums. After planting the garden, if you have some empty spaces, sprinkle some seeds of the old favorite mignonette toward the back of the bed and some annual candytuft in the foreground.

It is not necessary to have a herb garden to grow herbs, and although this may seem like heresy to the purist, I prefer to grow my herbs among the flowers. When I'm weeding or doing other garden chores and I brush against the herbs, they release their fragrant perfumes. Of the annual herbs, I always include basil – the purple-leaved 'Dark Opal' is very decorative. Tall lacy dill makes an excellent background plant in any flower border. I can't do without summer savory, simply because store-bought savory doesn't do a thing for my Christmas pork pie! The tender lemon verbena, rosemary and pineapple sage I grow in pots and bring indoors for the winter.

Some very fragrant summer flowering bulbs must be overwintered indoors. The ismene, *Hymenocallis calathina*, boasts large trumpet-shaped fringed blooms of white or yellow that blossom soon after planting. The bulb is easily stored at a temperature above 60°F (15°C). *Acidanthera* grows to a height of 3 feet (1 m) and the large sweet blooms are white with a maroon blotch. The tuberose's spikes of white blossoms smell exactly like gardenias.

From the many varieties of scented geraniums (pelargoniums), you will be able to find one to suit your nose. Their scents range from citrus through mints, spices, nuts, rose, balsam and eucalyptus. For hanging baskets, choose the small-leaved apple or the large velvet-leaved peppermint. For contrast against plain greens, choose the variegated 'Lady Plymouth' (a minty rose fragrance) or 'French Lace' (lemon). For upright plants that will assume shrub proportions in one season, choose 'Citronella' or a variegated rose-scented variety called 'Snowflake'.

Cosmos atrosanguineus appeals to chocoholics. The unmistakeable aroma of chocolate emanates from the rich burgundy blossoms. This native of Mexico, where it is now extinct, thrives in a hot sunny location. Unlike other cosmos, it does not produce seed and must be grown from cuttings. Technically a perennial hardy to Zone 7, the plant produces tubers that can be overwintered in a dormant state. However, this can be frustrating because the tubers tend to dry out and cuttings often succumb to mildew. I have found it best to grow this plant in a 10- to 12-inch (25 to 30 cm) pot as part of my potscaping. After frosts have stopped plant growth, I withhold water to induce dormancy. I store the tubers, still in the soil in the pot, in a cool place. Six to eight weeks before the last frost date, I move the pot to a warm, sunny spot and start watering to stimulate regrowth.

If you love to spend summer evenings cooling off on your patio or deck, you should include in your garden plants that are fragrant only at night.

The annual vine *Ipomoea alba* (moonflower) has fragrant large white blooms that open at dusk and close by noon the next day. Don't despair if you have poor garden soil, for this one performs best under these conditions. Soil that is too rich will result in all leaves and no blooms. Both the old-fashioned *Nicotiana* and *Matthiola bicornis*, night-blooming stock, an insignificant plant with mauve flowers, have extremely powerful scents. The little known *Pelargonium gibbosum* is a real conversation piece. It is best planted in a large pot with a small trellis to support its lanky stems. An old plant may reach several feet (one meter) in a pot. As it ages, every leaf node or joint becomes swollen, earning the name gouty geranium. But it does have two redeeming features: it has greenish yellow blooms that are very rare in the geranium world and these blooms are very sweetly scented — but only at night!

A selection of scented plants

Acidanthera

Antirrhinum majus (snapdragon)

Candytuft

Cosmos atrosanguineus

Datura

Heliotrope

Hymenocallis calathina

Ipomoea alba

Lathyrus odoratus (sweet pea)

Matthiola bicornis

Matthiola incana
   (sweet gillyflower)

Mignonette

Mirabilis jalapa (four o'clock)

Nasturtiums

Nemesia

Nicotiana

Pansies

Pelargoniums

Pelargonium gibbosum

Petunias (especially blue and
   purple varieties)

Sweet alyssum

Tuberose

Zaluzianskya capensis

The Contained Garden

Growing plants in containers is for everyone — from the gardener in a small city apartment to the owner of a large country estate, from the young- ster who plants his first half-barrel garden to the senior who cares for a window box because it doesn't require kneeling. When you grow plants in pots you get to know them very well, because they need regular attention and so are observed more closely than those planted in the garden.

Potscaping

The term "potscaping" has been coined to refer to the creative arrangement of plants in pots, just as "landscaping" refers to the arrangement of plants

DIVERSE FOLIAGE MAKES A LOVELY COMBINATION WITH, CLOCKWISE FROM RIGHT, TRAILING NASTURTIUM, *Pelargonium* 'VANCOUVER CENTENNIAL', *Lotus berthelottii*, *Leonitus leonurus*, AND VARIEGATED *Abutilon*.

grown in the ground. Penelope Hobhouse, a well-known English garden designer and writer, refers to her "jumble of pots," but potscaping can be much more artistic than a random collection of this and that.

A potscape can embrace all types of plants – annuals, houseplants summering outdoors, perennials waiting to be transferred to the garden, ornamental grasses, small shrubs, decorative vegetables, herbs and tender bulbs. It can be as few as three pots or as many as you like – truly a portable garden. When plants are flowering, those pots can be positioned in the foreground and then relegated to the background when the blooms are spent. Leftover annuals from spring planting may be kept in pots and planted in the garden later when an out-of-bloom perennial leaves a gap or a digging dog creates havoc. And a plant that is too special to be consigned to the general border, such as the beloved geranium that has been in the family for 36 years, will be the star attraction in a plant collection.

In a potscaping, the pots may be of varying sizes, but perhaps similar in design or construction, such as all wood or all clay. While the plants will also be diverse, there can be a unifying theme – perhaps all the flowers will be in shades of salmon pink to coral red, or silver plants will be used to tie the groups together, such as using *Helichrysum petiolare* to sprawl through neighboring pots.

A potscaping can be used to say welcome at your front door, to blur the edge of your patio and make it seem a part of the garden or to transform bare steps or a naked deck. Small groupings of three to five pots can add interest to patches of otherwise boring groundcovers. Remove one or two stones from a patio, and replace them with

POTSCAPING WITH ANNUALS

several interesting pots, planting some creeping thyme at the base. A grouping of pots placed along a balcony with wrought iron railings could contain lots of plants that will grow up the railings as well as trail over. This kind of potscaping will be enjoyed by passers-by so much more than just a hanging window box that looks like it's teetering on the brink.

When pots are grouped together, they stay cooler and require less water. Pots of plants in shady areas can be moved to sunny spots as needed to promote growth and set flower buds, and sun lovers can be moved to the shade during extreme heat.

When positioning hanging baskets, group three together at different heights instead of hanging just one. Don't make the mistake of hanging them so high you see only the bottom of the pot. Instead, keep them at nose and eye level where they can be fully enjoyed.

Containers

Plants can be grown in any container that holds soil and has drainage holes to allow excess water to escape — anything from old boots to bathtubs. Manufacturers offer a bewildering array to choose from in a variety of materials and sizes. Each has its own merits. Clay or terracotta is an excellent choice if watering daily is not a problem for you, for clay and terracotta dry out the most quickly. Soak the clay pot for an hour before planting to help alleviate this problem. Plastic pots offer better water retention, and manufacturers are slowly improving upon their utilitarian appearance. You also have the choice of wood, concrete and new lightweight styrofoam creations. Neutral colors and subdued designs offer the greatest flexibility

in plant choice. As for size, larger pots need watering less often than smaller ones. If you have a decorative container without drainage holes that you wish to use, place a utility pot that is slightly smaller in width and depth inside the decorative one. Stand it on a brick or upturned saucer so that excess water can drain away. Another solution is to drill drainage holes in the container — use an electric drill with a masonry bit for ceramic. Or use the pot without drainage holes for a miniature bog or water garden.

Soil

You will need a good commercially prepared potting mix or one made from your own recipe. Never use soil from the garden. Garden soil may contain weed seeds and carry fungal diseases, and it tends to become hard and impenetrable in small containers. The mix you use should contain a large proportion of peat moss to hold moisture and perlite to promote quick drainage and prevent soggy conditions. You can add some home-made compost, leaf mold or worm castings to your potting mix. At season's end, the used soil mix can be added to your garden or compost bin.

If your containers are very large, the cost of soil can be prohibitive. However, you can fill the bottom third with something other than soil mix. I suggest using leaves and prunings from your shrubs. These will eventually break down into valuable compost and cause the soil level to sink; the container should be topped up with fresh potting mix each spring.

Choosing suitable plants

Your first criteria is to select plants for sun or shade, depending on where your pots will be positioned. However, if you are willing to move pots according to the movement of the sun, you can choose any plants you fancy. If you opt for a portable garden, make the daily chore easier by displaying the pots in a wagon, wheelbarrow or tea cart.

The next criteria is height and habit (shape). Central or background plants need to be taller and of upright habit, while those near the edge should trail.

You can choose to have a pot full of the same plant, combine two or three different plants that complement each other or create an English cottage garden effect by planting one each of many different plants.

Don't skimp on the number of plants per pot. The pot should look almost full at planting time, so don't space plants as you would in a garden.

Planting technique

1. Almost fill a clean pot loosely with potting mix. Do not pack it down. Compare it to measuring ingredients for baking (the cup is loosely filled not packed, with flour). There is no need to add a drainage layer of stones or broken crockery. It is a myth that stones provide drainage, they don't. The holes provide drainage. (When was the last time you bought a professionally grown plant that had stones in the bottom?) If you are concerned about soil falling out of a large drainage hole, cover the hole with screening material or a paper coffee filter.

2. Into the top few inches (several centimeters) of soil, mix the recommended amount of balanced, slow-release granular fertilizer. The usual formulation is 14-14-14. It will break down gradually over the next three months.

3. Position the plants (still in their original pots) until you are satisfied with the arrangement.

4. Begin planting the central plants, or background plants if it's a window box. Remove them from their pots and loosen the root ball if the roots are pot-bound. Press the root ball firmly into the soil. The edging plants should be planted on a 45° angle or greater to induce them to trail or make an edge. Top with more soil if necessary, being sure to leave a 1-inch (2.5 cm) space between the soil line and top of the pot. This space should be completely flooded at each watering.

5. Pinch (remove) the growing tips of all plants to promote bushiness and therefore more blooms. This is probably the hardest part for beginners, but it really makes a difference later.

6. After watering well (that is, until water drains out the holes) place the pots in a sheltered location for a week or two until the roots become established. Do not hang baskets in a windy spot until they have become established.

Regular care

Plants in pots have different watering and fertilizing needs than plants in your garden. They need a commitment from you for regular care. Check your pots each day for moisture; each week, groom them, fertilize them and inspect them for pests. If you don't have time to work this into your schedule, your potscaping will not be successful.

Watering

Check containers every day, preferably at the same time. Water thoroughly when the soil feels dry to the touch. Use a watering can with a long spout. Remove the sprinkler head so that large amounts can be applied quickly. If you water with a hose, purchase a water breaker rather than a spray-gun attachment. A water breaker provides a gentle, thorough watering. Extension arms are available from 24 to 48 inches (60 to 120 cm) long — some even have a curved end for watering hanging baskets and window boxes that are positioned high overhead. On very hot windy days, it may be necessary to water twice. The alternative is to move the containers to a sheltered location out of direct sunshine for a few days — don't be concerned about their need for sunlight!

If water is scarce, place a saucer under each pot. Excess drainage water will be reabsorbed during the day (especially by clay pots). If water remains in the saucer by late afternoon, remove it. A poultry baster is a handy tool for this job. After heavy rains, be sure to empty saucers and decorative containers without drainage holes.

If one of your pots should dry so that the plants are at the wilting stage, plunge it into a tub of room-temperature water and leave it for 15 to 20 minutes. This allows the peat moss in the soil mix to absorb water and swell, expanding the soil ball to once again fill the pot. When the soil ball dries, it shrinks from the sides of the pot, leaving a space. If you water dried-out plants in the usual method,

the water runs right through and out the drainage holes. You may think you have given your plant enough water but in fact it has not penetrated the soil ball at all.

If you go away on holiday, make sure someone can check your pots for you, as well as watering the rest of your garden. To preserve moisture, dig a shallow depression in a shady spot and set the container in it. The earth will help keep the moisture in the soil cool, slowing down its evaporation.

Grooming

Groom your pots about once a week. This may require the use of a step ladder for hanging baskets, or maybe a pulley system for lowering them to eye level. Remove all spent blossoms, cutting back to the base of the flowering stem. If you just nip off the flowering heads, you will leave unsightly bare stalks. Cut back by half any plants that seem tired or bedraggled — most will become revitalized and bloom again in several weeks.

Pests

Check carefully for any insect pests. The most common are aphids, which are small, soft-bodied, pear-shaped creatures that cluster near growth tips and flower buds. They may be green, orange, black or woolly white. If tiny white insects fly up when you touch the plants, these are whiteflies. They cluster on the underside of the leaves. Both pests can be controlled by a spray of insecticidal soap to which the natural insecticide pyrethrum has been added. Be sure to follow directions carefully.

Fertilizer

After grooming and watering the plants, apply a diluted liquid fertilizer (fertilizer should never be applied to dry soil). Follow the directions on the package. For example, if the instructions are 1 tablespoon per gallon (15 mL per 4 L) once a month, then use ¼ tablespoon per gallon (4 mL per 4 L) once a week. Use a balanced formula (20-20-20) or one high in phosphorus (15-30-15). Containers need more fertilizer than plants in the garden because daily waterings leach away the nutrients.

End of Season

Make cuttings of your favorite plants to retain them for next year. (See page 152.) You will be tempted to bring your beautiful containers indoors when frost threatens. This is usually a disaster. Several factors — warmer night-time temperatures, drier air, less light — cause the plants' bottom leaves to drop, resulting in ugly bare stems. Unfortunately, insect pests often hitchhike indoors, causing problems with house-plants all winter.

If you have a small greenhouse, solarium or a large sunny window, you have good conditions for growing cuttings or you can cut the plants back to one-quarter their size and let them regrow with new foliage that is accustomed to indoor conditions.

A HANGING MOSS BASKET CONTAINING, CLOCKWISE FROM TOP, *Coleus* 'BURGUNDY COLUMNS', *Helichrysum* 'LIMELIGHT', *Glechoma hederacea*, *Coleus* 'DARK FRILLS' (SMALL LEAF), *Thunbergia battiscombei* (LARGE LEAF) AND OTHERS.

Moss Baskets

After growing plants in moss baskets for many years, I have developed a system that differs slightly from the usual recommendations. Some-times I fill a basket with just one or two types of plants, which can be very effective, but I prefer an entire garden in one container — full to the point of being blowsy (one plant per inch [2.5 cm] of basket diameter).

You will need a sturdy wire frame with chains for hanging. I prefer a shape with a flat bottom — this allows the basket to sit steady for planting and maintenance and increases the size of the soil ball. Fill the form loosely with moistened, long-fiber

WALL SCONCE CONTAINING, CLOCKWISE FROM TOP, COLEUS, *Ipomoea batatas* 'MARGUERITE', *Glechoma hederacea* (TRAILING), *Fuchsia megellanica aurea*, AND *Pelargonium* 'MADAME SALLERON'.

sphagnum moss. Plunge your hands into the center of the basket and push the moss to the sides — molding it to the frame and making sure that the top wire is well covered. The moss walls should be 2 inches (5 cm) thick. Place an aluminum pie plate or plastic saucer in the bottom to act as a water reservoir. An alternative is to purchase a basket with the moss preformed and then all you have to do is plunge it into a bucket of water for five minutes to moisten it. You can use coconut fiber instead of sphagnum moss, but it is difficult to cut through and not as easy to patch and restore.

Plan carefully before you start planting. It's a good idea to have a definite color scheme, perhaps all shades of pink, or a combination of cool blue and silver. I usually opt for a "Joseph's coat of many colors," but if you want this effect, you still must be sure to balance your colors. For example,

if you have a red upright, position another red in the composition at a different level. It is also important to balance plant size and weight: if you place a substantial cascading petunia on one side of the basket, there must be a large plant on the other side to act as a counterweight. For depth of color include some burgundy, black or purple foliage, like coleus, *Ipomoea batatus* 'Blackie', centradenia or plectranthus. Never place two variegated plants side by side.

Half-fill the basket with a good-quality, moist potting mix to which some compost or worm castings have been added. To plant the walls, I choose clingers — plants that will mold themselves to the moss and help to shade it, keeping the soil cool (sanvitalia, nemesia, creeping snapdragons, bacopa or any mounding plant, such as impatiens or fibrous begonias). I place one plant under each of the three to five handles to which chains will be attached, about halfway between the base and the top. Remove the plant from its pot. With your fingers gently open a hole in the moss wall so you can push the soil ball through. Pull the moss back around the neck of the plant. Spread the roots and cover them with soil. Trim the plant back so that new growth will assume the shape of the basket.

After planting the walls, fill the basket loosely with the soil mix (don't pack the soil down) and add a granular slow-release fertilizer, according to the manufacturer's suggestions. Then plant long trailers at the top edge of the basket, halfway between each clinger. These may be flowering plants: verbena, convolvulus, cascading petunias — or vining plants: vinca, ivy, *Glechoma* (creeping charlie), *Lamiastrum* (silver nettle) or lotus vine. Plant them on their sides, remembering to open the soil ball if the roots are potbound.

Next, plant the central area of the basket. I suggest one plant to creep through all the others to unify the whole arrangement, such as silver or gold helichrysum, *Anagallis* 'Skylover' or my favorite, *Bidens ferulifolia*. Add a vining plant that will attach itself to the chains and eventually camouflage them. It may even attach itself to the hook, which provides a permanent look. Try solanum, thunbergia, passion flower vine or asarina. In the central area there should be an upright substantial plant to provide fullness, something that will reach a height of at least 12 inches (30 cm): zonal geranium, upright fuchsia, dwarf marguerite daisy, B.C. begonia (*Begonia richmondensis*), coleus or heliotrope.

The planting is completed by adding edgers, plants that have a mounding or slightly trailing habit that will fill the space between the uprights and the trailers. To create the trailing effect, position the edgers at a 45° angle. There are a myriad of plants to choose from: small flowered *Abutilon*, *Centradenia*, *Brachyscome*, *Cuphea*, *Gazania*, *Felicia*, *Diascia*, etc.

When you have completed planting, pinch off all the growing tips to promote branching. You want the plants to weave through each other to make a unified whole rather than growing as individual plants in a basket. You can use cuttings from many of your houseplants to act as fillers and reduce costs. Spider plants, English ivy, wandering jew, geraniums, coleus, strawberry begonia and grape ivy are a few good choices.

After planting the basket, water it well and sit it in a lightly shaded, wind-free spot for two weeks until the roots are established. Then hang it in its desired location. It will be heavy, so be sure that the supports are strong. You will appreciate your efforts and find it easier to care for if you place it at eye level.

Moss baskets need to be monitored diligently. Even a couple of days' neglect can cause problems. Check your basket daily for moisture, and when watering, be sure to wet the moss as well as the soil. If your basket should ever dry out to the point of wilting, rehydrate it by plunging the entire basket into a tub of lukewarm water for 20 minutes. Allow it to sit in the shade for a day before rehanging. Water retention can be increased by placing a small sponge in the water reservoir before filling it with soil. For a large basket, sink a 4-inch (10 cm) plastic pot in the center of the basket and check that it is filled with water after each watering. Water-retaining crystals may be helpful, but they are expensive and can pose a problem if there is a heavy downpour or a wet season, when the soil will become waterlogged.

Each week, remove spent blooms and prune back any plant that may have temporarily finished blooming. A light pruning will encourage it to recharge so it will look good later in the season when something else is tired. During this weekly inspection, keep a watchful eye for insects. Aphids, whiteflies or spider mites are easy to control with insecticidal soap or a pyrethrum spray if they are not allowed to reach epidemic proportions. After watering and pruning, fertilize with a half-strength (15-30-15) liquid plant food (never add fertilizer to dry soil).

Your garden in a basket will not look the same all season. Just as in a garden, some plants will peak and wane, while others will be constants. Some will amaze — others may disappoint. If you want to keep a record of your moss basket's development, take monthly pictures and make notes. During an extreme hot dry spell, or while you are on vacation, take your basket down and set it in the shade.

In late summer, you can take some cuttings to grow during the winter for next year's basket. After the first frost, remove the plants and as much of the soil ball as possible. You will be able to reuse the moss next year, although it is a good idea to add some fresh moss each spring.

Strawberry Jars

A well-maintained strawberry jar cascading with flowers can be very satisfying, but many people give up on them after a season or two because they dry out so easily. Countless strawberry jars are collecting cobwebs in the back of potting sheds because of unsuccessful attempts to grow straw-berries, herbs or flowers in them.

Here are some suggestions for success:

1. If the jar is clay, be sure to soak it in water before planting (there are some good plastic look-alikes).

2. Plant from the bottom holes up, using small plants that will grow to fill their spaces.

3. In larger jars, position a perforated plastic tube in the center to facilitate watering.

4. Choose plants that are drought tolerant: portu-laca, Dahlberg daisy, sedums or sempervivums (hens and chicks).

5. An alternative that minimizes drying out is to plant a strawberry jar with violas and put it in the shade. Spent flowers must be removed weekly to keep the plants blooming.

6. For all clay strawberry pots, place a saucer under them so the clay will have a chance to absorb water and stay cool, the same way a clay wine cooler does.

CONTAINER GARDENS CAN BE MOVED AROUND THROUGHOUT THE SUMMER.

Recommended plants for containers

UPRIGHT PLANTS

Anisodontea

Abutilon (flowering maple)

Argyranthemum
   (marguerite daisies)

Begonia richmondensis and other
   upright types

Canna lilies

Coleus (upright forms)

Cheiranthus linifolium 'Variegatum' (wallflower)

Dahlia

Fuchsia (upright)

Geraniums (upright scented
   types)

Heliotrope

Ornamental grasses e.g.,
   Pennisetum rubrum

Phormium

Phygelius

*Salvia microphylla, S. patens,
   S. farinacea* 'Victoria'

TRAILING PLANTS

Asarina 'Bride's White',
   'Victoria Falls'

Bidens ferulifolia

Convolvulus sabatius

Glechoma hederacea variegata

Helichrysum petiolare (silver,
   gold or variegated)

Ivy geraniums

Lantana (trailing types)

Lobelia (trailing types)

Lotus berthelotii and *maculatus*

Petunia (cascading types: Wave,
   Surfinia, Supertunia, etc.)

Plectranthus

Rhodochiton (purple bells)

Solanum jasminoides 'Album'

Tradescantia (wandering jew)

Verbena (trailing types with lacy
   or broadleaf foliage)

Vinca major 'Variegata'

Viola hederacea

Wedelia trilobata

GOOD EDGES THAT SPRAWL

Abutilon 'Victory'

Antirrhinum
   (trailing snapdragon)

Bacopa

Brachyscome (Swan River daisy)

Centradenia

Coleus (trailing types)

Diascia

Fuchsia

Helichrysum bracteatum 'Golden
   Beauty'

Ipomea batatas 'Blackie'

Ipomea batatas 'Marguerite'

Laurentia axillaris

Lysimachia congestifolia 'Outback Sunset'

Mentha suaveolens
   (pineapple mint)

Monopsis lutea (golden lobelia)

Nemesia denticulata 'Confetti',
   'Innocence'

Petunia 'Million Bells'

Sanvitalia 'Golden Aztec'

Scaevola (fan flower)

Torenia 'Summer Wave'

THE
PLANTS

Cutting-Edge Annuals

Tender perennials grown from cuttings

In the last five years, a host of new plants grown from cuttings has appeared in North American markets, originating from European growers. Many garden centers refer to these plants as the "European annuals," although some have been developed as a result of plant breeding in Japan and Australia.

The process of growing plants from cuttings is known as vegetative propagation. New growing techniques and methods of transportation have made vegetative propagation a reliable option for professional growers. Now that plants have royalties and licensing rights, plant breeding is a lucrative business and growers are developing hundreds of new plants.

Computerization in all aspects of the growing process has improved efficiency and streamlined operations. Computer software programs have transformed record-keeping, greenhouse management, order processing and shipping. It is now possible to import new plant cuttings from around the world: within 24 hours unrooted cuttings of plants can be taken in one country, then shipped to another and planted in a rooting medium.

One company, Euro American Propagators in the United States, has offered some of these new plants under the banner Proven Winners (an excellent choice of words to encourage hesitant buyers!). This line is carefully controlled and named with new additions yearly and is available only from licensed propagators. But some nurseries import directly from German growers. Only the names are different. The tiny white-flowered bacopa from the Proven Winners line is called 'Snowflake', but you may see it sold as 'Snow Falls' or simply as white bacopa. This can be rather confusing.

Other trademark names you will see are Outback Plants and Cobitty Daisies. Cascading petunias are sold under several different names: Surfinia, Supertunia, Cascadia, Colgado and Solana Royals.

These cutting-grown plants are usually sold in 3- or 4-inch (7.5 to 10 cm) pots, or in hanging baskets in the same fashion as fuchsias, geraniums or New Guinea impatiens. Although they are usually recommended for containers, they also make excellent additions to perennial plantings. There are endless ways to incorporate them into your garden. Argyranthemums provide summer-long daisies in the flower border (perennial daisies bloom for only three to four weeks); bacopa will bloom all summer in a semi-shaded rock garden; convolvulus and diascia will brighten a sunny rock garden until the first frost. Heliotrope plants tucked among perennials near sitting areas fill the air with their delicate perfume. A new retaining wall planted with stephanandra or cotoneaster might look sparse for a full season, but if interplanted with bidens, it will soon be sporting billows of bright golden blooms.

The following list of new plants grown from cuttings will introduce you to some of these exciting new annuals. Start experimenting! But be warned: once you start, it's hard to stop.

Key to growing information in each plant entry

At the end of each entry on the following pages the optimum growing conditions and expected growth patterns are given for each plant. For example:

Light	Moisture/Soil	Growth Range
Sun/semi-shade	Average	6 in–4 ft (15 cm–1.2 m)

These are general guidelines only, and the conditions will sometimes change for different cultivars of the same plant. The term "drought resistant" applies to a plant planted in the ground; in a container, the same plant will need more regular watering. "Growth range" refers to the height of upright plants, and the length of sprawling or trailing plants. The range refers to all forms of the plant: if the range is given as 1–5 feet (30 cm–1.5 m), some types of the plant grow to 1 foot (30 cm) and others grow to 5 feet (1.5 m).

Abutilon x *hybridum*   is a shrubby, woody-stemmed plant, commonly called flowering maple in reference to the shape of its leaves. The bell-shaped flowers come in white, pink, apricot, yellow and shades of red. *A. pictum* 'Thompsonii' has green leaves splotched with gold and soft orange blooms; *A. savitzii* has creamy white leaves edged in green and only the occasional soft apricot blossom. These shrubs are often trained to tree form and they make excellent houseplants during the winter months. Pruning should be done just prior to the growth spurt in spring. The cultivar 'Moonchimes' is of shorter stature and can be grown in a large basket. *A. megapotamicum* and its hybrids produce more trailing stems and smaller blossoms, good for hanging baskets.

Abutilon 'MOONCHIMES'

Sun/semi-shade   Average   6 in–4 ft (15 cm–1.2 m)

Alonsoa meridionalis   'Fireball' is a delicate-looking plant originating in Peru, with burgundy stems, tiny leaves and bursts of small orange blossoms. Although pastels have been all the rage for a decade, bright colors are popular again and new orange flowers are blazing their way into our gardens and containers. At Hermanshof, in Weinheim, Germany, I saw an annual garden, approximately 50 feet by 6 feet (15 by 1.8 m), planted completely with flowers all in shades of orange. If you aren't sure how to handle orange, try combining it with blue. Alonsoa blooms best in cooler spots, so perhaps partial shade is the answer.

Sun/semi-shade   Average   6–18 in (15–45 cm)

Anagallis 'SKYLOVER'

Anagallis 'Skylover' is even bluer than the sky – it's an electric gentian blue that glows all summer. Upon closer observation, you'll notice that each small flower is centered with a splash of rosy-red, which can inspire some wonderful color combinations with surrounding plants. 'Skylover' is a selection grown from cuttings, but *Anagallis monelli* (syn. *A. linifolia*, *A. grandiflora*) is quite easily raised from seed. The plants grow from 10 to 18 inches (25 to 45 cm). They prefer light sandy soil and are happy edging a flower garden, tumbling over a retaining wall or scrambling through a rock garden. And 'Skylover' is a real joy in containers, where the stems become more pendulous, weaving through the other plants.

Sun/semi-shade   Average to dry   10–18 in (25–45 cm)

Angelonia, from Central and South America, is gaining acceptance as an interesting new
pot plant. With erect stems and narrow pointed
leaves, angelonia grows spikes of small, orchid-
like flowers that may be violet-blue, white or pink.

It combines well with heavier-foliaged plants like
Helichrysum petiolare.

Sun/semi-shade   Average   1–1½ ft (30–45 cm)

Anisodontea capensis, a small upright shrub of the *Malvaceae* family from South Africa, is sometimes referred to as South African mallow. The small three-lobed leaves and 1-inch (2.5 cm) wide soft pink blooms are in perfect proportion. This plant will happily thrive in your garden during the summer and move in to share your solarium in the winter. Requiring a sunny position and average moisture, it can be grown as a small shrub to a height of 2 to 3 feet (60 to 100 cm), or trained to a tree form.

Sun   Average   2–3 ft (60–100 cm)

Anisodontea IN COMBINATION WITH *Mimulus* (ORANGE) AND *Lavatera Maritima* (LARGE PINK BLOOM)

Antirrhinum majus 'LAMPION' WHITE

Antirrhinum majus are usually referred to as snapdragons in North America. The flower spikes range in height from 6 inches to 30 inches (15 to 75 cm), and the blooms open from the base to the top. The butterfly types have a more open-faced or cup-shaped bloom and are available in either single or double form. Snapdragons are cold tolerant and can be planted like pansies when the weather is still cool and will continue blooming until snow falls. An exciting innovation is the new trailing snapdragons for use in containers. The Lampion series has green foliage and bloom in white, yellow, salmon, pink and purple. 'Clownerie White' has silver foliage and is especially good for planting on the wall of a moss basket. The first bloom spike should be removed to promote branching, thus producing many more flowers.

Sun/semi-shade   Average   8 in–3 ft (20–100 cm)

47

Argyranthemum is for people who want daisies all summer long. Formerly *Chrysanthemum frutescens*, or marguerite daisies, they are still known in Europe as "Paris daisies" due to their popularity as cut flowers in that city. Originating in the Canary Islands, these daisies bloom non-stop from spring till fall. They combine well with perennials, make excellent container plants and can be trained to tree form. Overwintering is easy in a solarium or cool greenhouse, and new plants can be propagated from non-flowering shoots. Marketed under the Proven Winners banner are 'Butterfly', an excellent yellow at 14 to 18 inches (35 to 45 cm), and 'Dana', a slightly taller white. New introductions from the University of Sydney in Australia are called the Cobbity Daisies. Growing only 10 to 12 inches (25 to 30 cm) high, 'Sugar Baby' is a single white that does well in hanging baskets, while 'Sugar 'n Ice' is a slightly taller double white. The flowers of 'Sugar Buttons' are also double and smaller, but there are more of them. 'Summer Angel', white, and 'Summer Pink' reach 15 to 18 inches (37.5 to 45 cm). 'Summer Melody' has double pink flowers and the plant stays compact.

Sun/semi-shade   Average   10 in–3 ft (25–100 cm)

Bacopa 'SNOWSTORM'

Bacopa (botanically known as *Sutera cordata*) is truly a winner, whether it is used as a cascading edge in containers or planted in the garden. 'Snowflake' is an appropriate name for this plant with small dark green leaves covered with tiny white flowers. A recently introduced larger flowered version is named 'Snowstorm'. You may also see this plant labeled as 'Snow Falls' or simply White Bacopa. A lavender pink variety has a less compact habit and goes by the name 'Pink Domino' or 'Mauve Mist'. Bacopa thrives in semi-shade to full sun with regular watering (don't let it wilt!) but prefers a cool spot during our very hot summer days.

Sun/semi-shade   Average   2–12 in (5–30 cm)

Bidens ferulifolia 'GOLDIE'

Bidens ferulifolia was the first of the new European annuals to catch my attention. While traveling by bus through Germany en route to the 1993 IGA (International Garden Show) in Stuttgart, I kept seeing a small yellow flower that I couldn't identify. It was dancing through the window boxes full of traditional red geraniums, the long trailing stems giving a new dimension to what would otherwise be just blobs of color. Not until I reached the Container section of the show did I discover this to be *Bidens ferulifolia* — a spreading version of a seed-grown plant that I knew by the name of golden goddess, which grew to an upright 2 ½ feet (75 cm). Christened 'Goldmarie' by Proven Winners, bidens is a heat lover best used in mixed containers, where its trailing stems and ferny foliage find their way through other plants, pushing their bright yellow star-shaped blooms to the foreground. Growers who don't appreciate its sprawling habit will likely prefer the new compact variety called 'Goldie'. You may also find the smaller type under the name 'Samsara'. Bidens is an excellent "blooming until snowfall" edge for the flower garden or sprawler for the rock garden. An added bonus is that bidens happily self-seeds — often in the most cunning places. Just weed out the ones you don't want! Bidens requires little care. In a container it must be watered regularly but never allowed to sit in soggy soil. Planted in the ground it is amazingly drought-tolerant. It isn't necessary to deadhead religiously to promote bloom but if you want to achieve a compact shape you'll need to prune it back vigorously. I prefer the natural look.

Sun/semi-shade   Average   12–30 in (30–75 cm)

Brachyscome ʼJumbo Outbackʼ pink

'Ultra' is the name given to the Proven Winners selection.

Outback Plants has produced a grouping of nine different brachyscomes in colors ranging from white, yellow, pink and mauve to purple. They are referred to as mini-outback daisies and all sport the name ʼBillabongʼ. For example, ʼBillabong Sunburstʼ has pale green leaves and blooms that range from golden yellow to cream. The same company is promoting Jumbo Outback Daisies, developed from *Brachyscome multifida*, with a broader dark green leaf and a larger, 1 ½-inch (3.75 cm) diameter flower. They grow 15 to 20 inches (37.5 to 50 cm) tall and spread about 2 feet (60 cm). The color range varies between pink and shades of mauve.

Sun/semi-shade	Average	6–20 in (15–50 cm)

Brachyscome (often incorrectly spelled Brachycome) or Swan River daisy, forms mounds of needle-like foliage covered with lavender-blue daisies. There are several seed-grown varieties;

Bracteantha bracteata was formerly part of the genus *Helichrysum*, commonly known as strawflowers, grown from seed to be cut and dried as everlastings. The Proven Winner ʼGolden Beautyʼ is a strawflower grown from cuttings with a spreading habit that does extremely well in containers. The series of Outback Paper Daisies contains four different varieties ranging in height from 9 inches to 3 feet (22.5 to 100 cm). They require full sun, withstand high temperatures and prefer to be kept on the dry side. Butterflies love these bright everlasting strawflowers.

Sun	Average to dry	9 in–3 ft (22.5–100 cm)

Convolvulus sabatius (syn. *C. mauri-tanicus*), which you may find sold under the name Morning Trails, features small, light blue, morning-glory-like blooms covering long trailing stems of silvery green foliage. It grows on dry limestone rocks in northwest Italy, Sicily and northwest Africa. Convolvulus flowers from spring to fall, making it an excellent plant to hang over a wall, tumble through the rock garden or edge a large pot. It combines well with white or yellow-flowered plants. The spent blooms do not mar its beauty and there is no need for constant deadheading. Unfortunately the flowers close in the evening.

Sun/semi-shade   Drought resistant   2 ft (60 cm)

Diascia, a native of South Africa, is a member of the snapdragon family. The name is derived from *diaskeo*, meaning "to adorn." The common name, twinspur, refers to two horn-like spurs on each blossom. This tender perennial (hardy in Zone 7) is riding a wave of popularity. The color range includes every shade of pink and some mauves. The stems are lax, turning upright to lift the flowers into view. Spent blooms do not mar the beauty so there is no need for painstaking deadheading. It makes an excellent container plant in sun or semi-shade, especially in combination with silver *Helichrysum petiolare*, but I have also used it in a dry sandy rock garden in full sun where to my amazement it not only bloomed all summer but overwintered without any protection (in Zone 5) and performed beautifully the next summer as well!

Sun/semi-shade   Average to dry   6–12 in (15–30 cm)

Felicia amelloides *(bergeriana)*, which is sometimes referred to as blue Marguerite or kingfisher daisy, is a native of South Africa that provides an excellent blue for containers or complements perennials in the flower garden, in full sun to semi-shade. The yellow-centered blue daisies are held on wiry stems well above the small, almost succulent foliage. There is also a white-flowered variety. Even more exciting is the variegated form: green leaves widely bordered with cream, topped with blue flowers. Another form has very narrow leaves – the mature plant resembles an asparagus fern that has decided to produce blue daisies. My favorite way to use felicia is to plant it on the side of a moss basket. The foliage hugs the wall while the stems turn upright, showing the flowers to good advantage. Regular deadheading and pinching back the growing tips promotes new growth and lots of bloom.

Sun/semi-shade   Average   6–12 in (15–30 cm)

Fuchsia has increased in popularity in direct relation to the increased interest in hummingbird gardens because the little "hummers" find fuchsia irresistible! I always have fuchsia in a hanging basket outside my kitchen window so the hummingbirds and I breakfast together.

Wild fuchsias found in Central and South America, the West Indies and New Zealand have a simple two-part flower consisting of sepals (petals) and a protruding corolla (tube). Sometimes these two parts are the same color but usually they are different.

The species *F. magellanica* is hardy to Zone 7 (worth a try in Zone 6). Along the coast of southern Ireland, hardy fuchsia are grown as tall hedges. However, most cultivars are tender and must be wintered indoors in a cool bright place where they are not allowed to dry out completely.

Extensive hybridization has produced huge blowsy flowers up to 6 inches (15 cm) in diameter. These are best typified by the California Dreamer series. Some cultivars have proven to be heat resistant, which is good news for those of us who have hot summers, since fuchsias generally prefer cool, moist, partially shaded locations. Cultivated forms have a range of plant habits from prostrate, semi-trailing or bushy to very upright. The upright forms are easily trained to become small trees. Flower size may be as small as ¼-inch (25 mm) and colors consist of red, pink, purple, orange and white or combinations of these. Leaf color is usually mid- to dark green but may be gold, burgundy or variegated, as in the cultivar 'Tom West' with its pink, white and green foliage. It is now possible to obtain hybrid fuchsia seed that flowers 14 weeks from sowing. Several varieties are available, including 'Florabelle' and 'Fête Floral'.

Weekly deadheading is important if you wish to keep your fuchsias blooming all summer. Withered petals will drop off by themselves, leaving the small cherry-like fruit that contains the seeds. If left on the plant, it will ripen to a deep red and can be used to make fuchsia pie. You can find a recipe in *The Edible Ornamental Garden* by John E. Bryan and Coralie Castle (101 Productions, San Francisco, 1974). They write, "It has a unique flavor and like rose hips, [the fuchsia fruit] should be combined with cornstarch to temper the slightly astringent taste." I prefer to deadhead the flowers to ensure continuous blooms.

Semi-shade	Average	1–2 ft (30–60 cm)

Heliotropium arborescens (syn. *H. peruvianum*) was a popular conservatory plant, known as cherry pie, in the Victorian era. My nose interprets the fragrance as cream soda, but others liken it to baby powder. Now heliotrope is enjoying a resurgence of popularity, as are other Victorian favorites. One species, available as a cutting-grown plant, has fragrant white blooms that become soft blue as they age. Easier to find are the blue/purple forms with large broccoli-like heads of flowers, sold under the names 'Fragrant Beauty' and 'Marine'. Watch for a new trailing form called 'Iron Gate'. The foliage is coarse deep green and turns darker when grown in cool conditions. I love to grow heliotrope in a mixed hanging basket hung at nose level. In the garden, sandy loam soil suits it best. Heliotrope grow to 18 inches (45 cm) in one season, but they can be trained to 3-foot (100 cm) standards or pillars (upright bushes usually supported in a cage) in two years. Water regularly and feed it well during summer months — heliotrope does not bounce back well from drying out, but doesn't like to be water-logged either.

Sun/semi-shade   Average to moist   18 in (45 cm)

Impatiens are relative newcomers to the garden scene. Since their introduction about 30 years ago, they have become the most widely grown annual because they flower so well in shady sites. Unfortunately, they are often overused, but a few impatiens, situated among ferns and other shade-loving perennials, couldn't be prettier.

The mass-produced single-flowered impatiens are grown from seed, while the double-flowered rosebud types and the New Guinea hybrids are usually produced from cuttings. The New Guineas are often referred to as sunshine impatiens because they are happy in the full sun. Their decorative value extends beyond their large, luminous blooms to their deep green, almost burgundy leaves. Some have variegated green and cream foliage.

The Seashell series, also grown from cuttings, has been introduced recently. Breeders finally succeeded in incorporating the yellow flowering gene into the garden impatiens, producing a series with color ranging from yellow through apricot to orange. The flowers are shell-shaped and are well suited for the garden or containers.

Sun/semi-shade   Average to moist   6–18 in (15–45)

Impatiens 'Seashell' Yellow

Lantana camara is native to the tropical areas of North and South America. It's a shrubby plant growing 3 to 6 feet tall (100 to 180 cm), with wrinkled leaves that have a pungent fragrance when crushed. The clusters of flowers are yellow to orange, turning red with age. Butterflies love the nectar but all parts of the plant are poisonous to humans. Some people experience a mild allergic reaction from handling the foliage. There is a spreading form, *Lantana montevidensis*, which has pale magenta flowers. Many cultivars of lantana have evolved from these tropicals. The upright form has colors ranging through all shades and combinations of white, yellow, orange, pink and red and are very effective trained to tree form. The trailing types are available in white, soft yellow and mauve. They thrive in hot locations and are excellent container plants.

Sun	Average	10–24 in (25–60 cm)

Lavatera maritima is a shrub native to Spain and the western Mediterranean, where it blooms from February to June and again in autumn, thriving in poor dry soil and sunny hot weather. The flowers are beautiful, large and soft pink with purple throats, but it also has spectacular silky gray-green foliage. Position this one where you can stroke its leaves. Do not treat this plant with kindness — it thrives on tough love! Too-rich soil and plenty of moisture will result in lush foliage and no flowers. This plant definitely blooms better when it is slightly stressed, so fertilize sparingly and water only enough to keep it from wilting.

| Sun | Drought tolerant | 2–3 ft (60–100 cm) |

Leonitis leonurus (syn. *Leonitis ocymifolia*), known as lion's tail, is a herbaceous perennial native to South Africa. In its natural habitat, it grows on the edge of rough grasses where there is adequate moisture, reaching a height of 6 feet (1.8 m). In cultivation, because it is pinched to promote bushiness, expect a height of 4 feet (1.2 m) and bloom in late summer and autumn. It is reported to survive winters of 14°F (-10°C) if the roots are protected by mulch. Otherwise overwinter in a pot in the greenhouse or solarium.

The whorls of tubular velvety orange blooms are amazing. In South Africa, the plant is used as a folk remedy to produce a mild euphoric effect. I feel euphoric just looking at it!

| Sun | Average to moist | 3–5 ft (1–1.5 m) |

Lobelia ricardii, the popular little blue-flowered container plant, originated in the Cape of Good Hope. This new, vegetatively grown form of lobelia comes in two shades of blue and is more reliable for continued summer bloom than the seed-grown *L. erinus*. It copes beautifully with sun and heat. Each bloom of the double form called 'Kathleen Mallard' looks like a little double blue rose. Be advised that 'Kathleen' is very unforgiving if her water needs are not met exactly — neither too much nor too little! *L. erinus* is grown from seed in both compact and trailing forms in shades of blue, carmines and white. Because it prefers full sun and cool temperatures, it is best placed in partial sun where it has protection from midday heat. Ample moisture is necessary. It has a tendency to die out in mid-summer. At the first sign of browning, cut the plant back halfway and it will likely regenerate.

Sun/shade   Average to moist   12–18 in (30–45 cm)

Lotus maculatus

Lotus berthelotii   and *Lotus maculatus*
are silvery cascading sub-shrubs native to Tenerife
but now rarely found in the wild. They are very similar, with long trailing stems of feathery foliage.
L. maculatus has flatter, wider leaves and yellow
flowers with a brown stripe. *L. berthelotii* has nar-
rower leaves and bright red and black flowers. The
common name, parrot's beak, describes the shape
of the flower. From a *Berthelotii* x *maculatus* cross
come two new cultivars, 'Amazon Apricot' and
'Amazon Sunset', with blooms in shades of orange.

This plant flowers in late winter in a cool solarium
or greenhouse and continues flowering until early
summer. Although the curious blooms are much
appreciated, this plant provides a valuable silver
accent even when not flowering. Make sure it gets
sufficient moisture; if lotus gets too dry, it sheds
its leaves.

Sun/semi-shade   Average to moist   18–30 in (45–75 cm)

Mimulus aurantiacus (syn. *M. gluti-nosus*), propagated from cuttings, is very different from the mimulus or monkey flower grown from seed. It has sticky dark green leaves and soft orange flowers and is a native of Oregon and California, growing in dry, well-drained soil in rocky places and open woodland. There are several closely related species: *M. longiflorus*, with blooms of buff, yellow or orange; *M. puniceus*, with red flowers; and *M. bifidus*, with creamy white flowers. Several hybrids have been produced: 'Verity Purissima' (white), 'Verity Buff', 'Verity Caroline' (yellow) and 'Verity Magenta', Mimulus is very popular in England and will now undoubtedly follow the usual route of returning to North America. It makes an excellent container plant, especially in mixed baskets, where some stems tend to grow upwards while others trail down.

Sun/semi-shade   Average to dry   12–18 in (30–45 cm)

Mimulus aurantiacus

Nemesia 'CONFETTI'

Nemesia refers to a genus of plants from South Africa that includes annuals, perennials and shrubs. *N. strumosa* is the commonly grown garden annual with multi-colored flowers. Recently, varieties that are tender perennials have been introduced, and they make excellent garden or pot plants. They have masses of small, trumpet-shaped flowers that bloom all summer. Colors range from white to shades of pink and smoky blue. My current favorite is 'Confetti', a lavender-pink nemesia with the fragrance of lilacs. Two of the latest introductions are 'Compact Innocence', with fragrant white blooms, and 'Bluebird', with dusky blue flowers.

Sun/semi-shade   Average   12 in (30 cm)

Osteospermum 'MIRA'

Osteospermum or African daisy is a tender perennial that performs best in full sun and cool temperatures, sometimes refusing to bloom during the summer's intense heat. It is available in white or yellow and shades of pink and mauve, but it is the blue center that makes this daisy so special. The darker reverse petal color becomes noticeable when the flower closes on dull days and in the evening. Some varieties have spoon-shaped petals, creating a very exotic effect. 'Silver Sparkler' has green and cream variegated foliage. Spent flowers should be removed regularly to ensure continued bloom.

Sun   Average to dry soil   12 in (30 cm)

62

Pelargonium Domesticum 'Sweet Memory'

Pelargoniums (Tender Geraniums)

Don't be upset if you have problems with the botanical name of these old favorites — you're not the first. Linnaeus, the taxonomist who established the system of naming plants using Latin names, made the original error that resulted in the confusion. In the 17th century when some new plants arrived in Europe from South Africa they were called geraniums because the flowers resembled the *Geranium pratense,* or the meadow cranesbill of the fields and roadsides. Linnaeus classified them as geraniums. Later botanists realized basic differences in the flower structure, and they were renamed *Pelargonium*. But everyone still called them geraniums! Only recently has this presented a problem. With the growing interest in perennials, the true, hardy geranium has catapulted into popularity. Now, when someone says "geranium" we must ask if they are referring to the tender geranium (pelargonium) or the hardy geranium (cranesbill). Very similar to the geraniums and pelagoniums are the erodiums. Slight differences in flower structure earned them their own classification.

Sun/shade   Average   3–36 in (7.5–100 cm)

Members of the Geraniaceae Family

Geraniums (Cranesbill) — Hardy
Pelargonium (Storksbill) — Tender
Erodium (Heronsbill) — Some tender, some hardy

The geraniums you see on windowsills are correctly *Pelargonium* x *hortorum*, a hybrid between *P. zonale* and *P. inquinans*. From the original cross have come hundreds of hybrids, often referred to as zonal geraniums. Each year several new cultivars are offered for sale. In order to make room for these new ones, some cultivars must be dropped. A new introduction from several years ago may now be listed as "no longer in cultivation." Cultivars that were widely grown 20 years ago, such as 'Crimson Fire', are now considered heirlooms. The new pelargonium cultivars tend to be more compact, with a uniform growth rate, rich green leaves and large flower heads. The individual florets are often blotched with a contrasting color. These newcomers are so perfect that they almost appear artificial. I remember fondly the tall, rangy geraniums that grew on my grandmother's farmhouse windowsills, filling the windows with large velvety leaves and bright red blooms.

The recent interest in all things Victorian has caused a revival for the fancy-leaf types (see Flamboyant Foliage) and the ones with scented leaves (see Fragrance in the Garden).

Zonal pelargoniums are propagated from stem cuttings. Only licensed growers are allowed to propagate the new cultivars and royalties are paid for each cutting that is grown. The introduction of F1 hybrids grown from seed has provided another option for both professional and amateur growers. An F1 hybrid is a plant derived from man-made crosses (pollination by hand) for several generations. Seed produced by these hybrids may revert to any of the ancestors. Unfortunately, the F1 pelargonium hybrids are limited to varieties with single blooms.

Collectors of miniatures will be happy to know that there are now dozens of diminutive cultivars of pelargoniums, ranging in height from 3 to 8 inches (7.5 to 20 cm) at maturity, available from specialty nurseries. They are perfect for growing under fluorescent lights or on a sunny windowsill. When these plants are several years old, they develop woody stems and look like little trees — transfer them to shallow pots and you have "bonsai" (not true bonsai, of course!).

Long popular in Europe, pillars of pelargoniums will soon start appearing in North American potscaping designs. Nurseries are ready to offer gardeners a new zonal geranium called 'Pillar Salmon', a pillar geranium with an extremely vigorous upright growth habit suitable for growing in a tomato cage, decorative obelisk or tied to a trellis. A small plant will produce a 3-foot (1 m) pillar in four months.

Another Victorian favorite showing signs of revival is the *P. domesticum* group. These 'Martha Washington' or regal geraniums have blooms resembling azaleas. The mini-regal or angel group have smaller flowers, like pansies. These are best treated as a blooming pot plant, available in late winter and early spring. They usually do not continue blooming through summer's heat because they require cool night-time temperatures (below 60°F/15°(C) to set flower buds. Ian Gillam of

Vancouver, a pelargonium enthusiast, has developed two cultivars that do perform well as summer bedding plants. He named them 'Sweet Memory' and 'Sweet Success' in honor of Robert Sweet, known for his early botanical sketches of pelargoniums.

The ivy geraniums, *P. peltatum*, usually only grown in containers, are also effective planted in rock gardens and trailing over retaining walls. They need protection from hot midday sun. Able to withstand more sun and heat are the single flowered Balcons or Cascade series, used extensively in European window boxes.

The Stardom series with names such as Elizabeth or Marilyn are floribundas — zonal and ivy crosses with leaves like zonals and spreading habits like ivies. They bloom profusely with smaller flower heads than regular zonals making them excellent candidates for mixed containers.

Pelargonium peltatum 'BALCON' PINK STAR

Pelargoniums can be overwintered in several ways.

1. Take stem cuttings several weeks before frost is expected.

2. Cut plants back to approximately a quarter of their height and pot them to regrow in a sunny windowsill. Bringing a large plant from the garden to your living room at summer's end is disastrous — lower light, lower humidity and warmer nighttime temperatures cause serious leaf drop.

3. If you have a dark cold room or wine cellar where the temperature is just above freezing, you might consider digging the mature plant, shaking the soil off the roots, and storing it bareroot. If the room has high humidity, it will keep the roots from drying out, or you can cover them with moist peat moss. This is the method used by nursery professionals to keep woody deciduous plants over the winter. Six to eight weeks before the last frost date, cut back the top and the roots to 4 to 6 inches (10 to 15 cm), soak them for a few hours in lukewarm water and plant them in a 6-inch (15 cm) pot. Water well and place in a sunny window. Do not water again until new growth appears and the soil surface is dry to the touch.

Petunias sometimes have the reputation of being slightly "ho-hum." I must confess that prior to seeing Surfinia petunias for the first time in Belgium in 1993, I was of this opinion. But these new vegetatively grown petunias were cascading 2 to 3 feet (60 to 100 cm) out of the window boxes, creating lovely blankets of bloom. You can find these new petunias under many names, including Surfinia, Supertunia, Cascadia, Colgado and Solana Royals.

Petunias are actually tender perennials, which were regularly grown from cuttings in the 19th century before plant breeders were able to stabilize the different colors when growing from seed. The problem of viruses infecting stock plants has been corrected by improved nursery techniques, but if you should ever see a petunia with deformed foliage, it should be destroyed immediately.

Cutting-grown petunias are usually planted in containers, where they will trail 3 or 4 feet (100 to 120 cm), but they can also be used among new perennial plantings to provide a carpet while the perennials are getting established.

Petunias are heat tolerant, performing best when it is over 65°F (18°C). They can be grown in full sun or semi-shade and should be allowed to dry slightly between thorough waterings (but don't let them wilt). Young petunias must be pinched several times to create full bushy plants. Only three or four plants are needed to create a luxuriant 12-inch (30 cm) hanging basket. They are heavy feeders and need regular fertilizing, augmented with monthly applications of chelated iron. Watch for new developments in this exciting plant group — we'll soon have the color yellow and double forms as well.

Recently, a new tiny-flowered petunia has been introduced under various trade names, including Million Bells and Liricashower Petunias. Botanists feel they really belong in their own genus called *Calibrachoa*. These plants are more compact, with twiggy stems, tiny slender leaves and masses of nickel-sized blooms. They are best used in containers, where just three will fill a 10-inch (25 cm) basket. They produce a mounded rather than a trailing effect. "Petitunias" are midway in size between the calibrachoas and the regular vegetative types of petunias.

| Sun/semi-shade | Average | 6–36 in (15–100 cm) |

Phygelius, although discovered in South Africa over 100 years ago, are only now becoming popular. These bushy, upright plants produce prominent spikes of downfacing tubular blooms from mid-summer to frost. Hummingbirds find them irresistible. Deadheading keeps the plants tidy and producing profusely. Their common name is Cape fuchsia and they prefer a warm, sunny location in moist but well-drained soil. These Zone 8 perennials will overwinter in mild areas but for much of North America they are best treated as container plants that can winter indoors. There are two original species: *P. capensis*, which has orange-red blooms positioned around the flower spikes, and *P. aequalis*, which has soft pink blooms on one side of the spike all facing in the same direction. The first hybrid, *P. x rectus* 'African Queen', had bigger spikes of red flowers. Peter Dummer, of Hillier Nurseries in England, developed the lemon yellow form, *P. aequalis* 'Yellow Trumpet' in 1973. The following varieties are highly recommended: *P. x rectus* 'Devil's Tears' — deep red blooms; *P. x rectus* 'Winchester Fanfare' — pale dusky red tubes with scarlet lobes; *P. x rectus* 'Moonraker' — soft lemon yellow blooms; *P. x rectus* 'Salmon Leap' — orange blooms; and *P. x rectus* 'Trewidden Pink' — dusky pink blooms. Mature plants can grow to 4 feet (1.2 m) tall and 4 feet wide (1.2 m).

Sun   Average to moist   4 by 4 ft (1.2 by 1.2 m)

Portulaca grandiflora

Portulaca grandiflora, grown from seed has for years been a favorite to brighten dry locations through long hot summers, often self-seeding and returning to bloom yet again in a marvelous mish-mash of colors. The Sundial series at last gave the discerning gardener a choice of separate colors. Now we have two further choices in vegetatively grown portulaca, which can be used in containers or in the garden. The large flowered type has huge blooms in rose, white or a pink-white bicolor on stems that trail 18 inches (45 cm). *P. oleracea* (purslane) has delightful small blooms in colors of white, yellow, apricot, pink and red. It is the perfect answer for what to grow in the clay strawberry jar where everything else you tried turned crispy brown by midsummer. It's also an excellent plant for late summer bloom in an otherwise green rock garden. The flowers close at dusk or on cloudy days.

Sun	Drought resistant	2 in (12-in spread)
		(5 cm/30 cm spread)

Salvia encompasses many different types of plants, some cold-tolerant, some frost-tender, some grown for their fragrant foliage (sage), others for their bright blooms (*S. splendens*). Many are seed-grown, but the following are propagated from cuttings.

S. greggii, a short shrubby plant with small leaves and red, purple, pink or white flowers, is easily grown in dry, sunny places. *S. microphylla* (syn. *S. grahamii)* is a spreading shrub that grows to 3 feet (1 m) and flowers continuously from early summer to heavy frost with pink or red blooms. *S. leucantha*, a late summer and fall bloomer, sports velvety gray-green foliage and purple to mauve flowers. In milder areas, it is a perennial. For those in colder climes, the plants can be cut back and overwintered in a greenhouse or propagated by cuttings. Another tender perennial is *S. guaranitica*, with large flowers in shades of deep blue that sometimes grow to 9 feet (2.7 m). *S. patens* can be grown from seed or cuttings. 'Cambridge' has pale blue flowers; 'Oxford', deep blue; 'Chilcombe', pale lilac; and 'Alba', white. This native of Mexico forms tuberous roots that can be dug and overwintered like a dahlia.

S. uliginosa grows from 5 to 6 feet (1.5 to 1.8 m) tall and flowers from mid-summer to autumn, with small blue flowers at the ends of tall arching stems. It prefers moist soil, unlike other salvias.

Sun   Average to dry   1–5 ft (30–150 cm)

Salvia patens 'CAMBRIDGE'

Sanvitalia, or creeping zinnia, has in the past been grown from seed and used as a ground-cover, an edge or a low rockery plant. Masses of tiny lemon, gold or orange single zinnia-like flowers cover short spreading plants. Now a burgundy-stemmed sanvitalia is being propagated from cuttings and proving itself excellent for use in containers. I particularly like to use it planted into the wall of a moss hanging basket.

Sun/semi-shade   Average   4 by 12 in (10 by 30 cm)

Scaevola aemula, or blue fan flower, from Australia, was the first of the new container plants to catch the attention of the gardening public. The patented Proven Winners variety is called 'New Wonder'. This semi-trailing plant loves summer heat, tolerating temperatures to 104°F (40°C) without experiencing a stoppage in bloom.

However, it is adversely affected by drying out or soggy soil. An occasional application of chelated iron will keep the foliage dark green and result in deeper colored flowers. You may also see mauve-, pink- or white-flowered versions.

Sun/semi-shade　　　Average　　　12–18 in (30–45 cm)

Torenia fournieri 'SUMMER BLUE WAVE'

Torenia fournieri, a native of the tropical woodlands of Asia and Africa, is well-suited for semi-shaded spots in our gardens when grown from seed. The tubular, two-lipped blooms are available in white, pink, blue and mauve, usually with yellow-marked throats. Proven Winners has introduced *T. f.* 'Summer Blue Wave', now propagated from cuttings. This upright annual will form a nicely mounded pot in the semi-shade or can be combined with coleus, small-leaved helichrysum and fuchsia for a pretty mixed basket.

Semi-shade   Average to moist   8 in (20 cm)

Verbena peruviana, a native of South America, is a delightful plant to trail over the edges of containers or to tumble over retaining walls and scramble through rock gardens. It is amazingly drought tolerant. In containers it should be allowed to dry slightly between thorough waterings as it resents being soggy. To form bushy plants with lots of bloom, cut back the growing tips several times when the plants are young. Because verbena can survive several degrees of frost, it keeps blooming until freeze-up.

Trailing verbena can be divided into two groups. One, christened 'Tapien' by Proven Winners, has delicate lacy foliage and smaller heads of bloom in soft pink, blue, lavender or violet-blue. The other type has deep green broader leaves and softball-sized flower heads in bright pink, red and violet. Proven Winners calls these 'Temari,' which means "handful of flowers." You will see both these types of verbena sold under many different names. 'Homestead Purple', a cultivar of the large-leaf type, has long been a favorite of mine for both containers and gardens.

Sun   Drought resistant   1–2 ft (30–60 cm)

Verbena 'TEMARI' RED

Tender Bulbs

Plants that grow from underground storage organs — bulbs, tubers, corms and rhizomes (sometimes grouped under the term geophytes) — can be divided into two groups: winter hardy (tulips) and tender (dahlias). Some, such as Montbretia (syn. Crocosmia), are best described as borderline: hardy to Zone 7 and sometimes colder when covered with a thick mulch. Hardy bulbs are planted in great numbers, but tender bulbs are often scorned because they must be dug up in the fall. Unfortunately, many gardeners miss the exhilarating sense of harvesting bulbs each autumn. I love to dig up a huge canna that began as a small rhizome and is now large enough to share with a friend, or to discover a handful of oxalis bulbs that developed from just a few.

If digging up the bulbs each fall is a problem, plant tender bulbs in pots. When they are in leaf, they add body to your "potscaping"; when in flower, they will produce some of your most exotic blooms. If blooming is late, you can move the pots indoors to enjoy them for a few more weeks. When frosts close down the garden, stop watering the pots of bulbs and store them in the basement. Do not remove the foliage until it turns brown. Next spring simply resume watering, and when the bulb begins growing start a liquid fertilizing regime. Many bulbs prefer to be potbound and will bloom better the second and third year (agapanthus is a good example). Some will often start to regrow without any encouragement from us (for example, agapanthus, cannas, eucomis) while others (such as caladiums and tuberous begonias) need a burst of heat to get started. These you will likely decide to repot.

Alternatively, you can treat the inexpensive types as annuals and buy new ones each year. Whatever you do, don't overlook these wonderful plants – try at least one new variety each year – you'll be rewarded with exotic flowers, flamboyant foliage or heady perfume.

Remember the basics concerning bulbs. The leaves need fertilizing while they are growing and making food. Never cut off green leaves before they've had a chance to store the food in the bulb. Always let the leaves turn brown before removing them. In the traditional dig-and-store treatment, be sure to allow several days of curing time. To cure bulbs, spread them in a warm dry place with good air circulation so the skins can toughen before storage. Some people hesitate to experiment with tender bulbs because they don't have a cold basement for overwintering, but tender bulbs are tropical plants and need only cooler temperatures for their winter dormant period. Often a dark cupboard on an outside wall will be just perfect.

Although referred to generally as "bulbs," bulbs, corms, tubers and rhizomes each have their own particular characteristics and require different treatment. A true bulb is a bud on a shortened stem surrounded by scale-like leaves that contain stored food (agapanthus is a true bulb).

A corm resembles a bulb, but a bud at the top of a solid stem produces flowers and leaves and lateral buds to form small offsets (gladiolus is a corm). Each corm is used up during the season's growth and a new corm is produced for the following year.

A tuber is a swollen root used for food storage (dahlia is a tuber).

A rhizome is a swollen horizontal stem just below the soil's surface (canna is a rhizome). Roots grow downward from its underside while the growth tip produces the new plant.

Achimenes   is known as the "hot-water plant" because it needs watering with warm water. This member of the gesneriad group has furry leaves that can become disfigured by cold water. Place several of the tiny pine-cone-like rhizomes in a 4- or 5-inch (10 to 12 cm) pot eight to twelve weeks before the last frost date. Masses of velvety tubular blooms in rich shades of red, pink, blue, purple or white will be produced all summer. Do not allow them to dry out as wilted foliage never completely revives. This is a perfect pot plant for a verandah or balcony in semi-shade. In autumn, stop watering to induce dormancy. Store cool and dry over the winter.

Semi-shade   Average to moist   6–10 in (15–25 cm)

Acidanthera bicolor   has been reclassified as *Gladiolus callianthus* but is still sold under its original name. It has sword-shaped leaves that reach a height of 3 feet (1 m) and 3-inch (7.5 cm) fragrant white blooms with deep purple throats that appear in autumn. Earlier flowering can be encouraged by starting the corms indoors six weeks before the last frost date. In our climate, this native of tropical Africa often does not have time to produce large enough corms to make overwintering worthwhile. Fortunately, they are inexpensive and make a wonderful addition to the autumn garden. They also make an effective central plant in a large container.

Sun/semi-shade   Average   3 ft (1 m)

Agapanthus, known as "lily of the Nile," produce large heads of bloom in shades of blue or white from mid-summer to fall. Strap-shaped leaves vary in width and height according to varieties. Agapanthus need a good root structure before blooming so they are best grown in pots, which can be plunged into the ground if desired. They are easily moved indoors for the winter where the foliage may stay green. If it does stay green, water lightly once a month to prevent complete drying out. A cool solarium or greenhouse would be an ideal resting place. If the leaves die back, stop watering until spring.

| Sun | Average | 18–36 in (45–100 cm) |

Amaryllis belladonna blooms in the fall with six or more large fragrant flowers atop a stout 1- to 3-foot (30 to 100 cm) stalk. After flowering, glossy strap-shaped leaves remain green until spring. This bulb can be used where needed for a burst of autumn interest. The *Amarcrinum* (*Amaryllis* x *crinum*) has similar fall flowers but the foliage stays green all year, making it an excellent winter solarium plant.

Sun   Average   1–3 ft (30–100 cm)

Anemone coronaria, the "poppies" of the bulb world, are hardy to Zone 7. In colder areas, they should be planted in the spring. The tubers are hard, dry and shriveled and must be soaked overnight in lukewarm water before planting. The plants grow 12 to 18 inches (30 to 45 cm) tall and flower colors are red, white or blue. Blooms last longer if the plants are positioned in dappled or midday shade.

Semi-shade   Average   12–18 in (30–45 cm)

Begonias that grow from tubers are classified according to their flower shapes. The double-flowered types may be of rose, camellia or carnation form. The smaller-flowered non-stop begonias, which carry their upfacing flowers above the foliage, are grown from seed but do make small tubers by summer's end. The single-flowered picotees have a contrasting color on the edge of the petals. Pendula forms have a trailing habit suitable for hanging baskets.

Technically, a tuberous begonia grows from a tuber-corm. It is disc-shaped, with several buds on the upper surface and roots growing from the bottom surface. These increase in size each year.

Buy the tubers as soon as they are available in the stores (they tend to deteriorate quickly in a dry atmosphere). As with all bulbs, choose the largest, heaviest ones. Keep them cool until planting time, six to eight weeks before the last frost date in your area. If little pink buds are not visible on the tubers or the tubers seem shriveled, soak them overnight in lukewarm water before planting. Nestle the tubers into a moist soilless mix in a small pot with the concave side up. Do not cover with the soil mix until the new shoots are 2 inches (5 cm) tall. Warm soil will hasten shoot growth. When the shoots are about 3 inches (7.5) tall, transfer them to 4- or 5-inch (10 to 12 cm) pots. Grow them in a bright sunny location or under fluorescent lights. If the plants become too tall, cut off the top 3 inches (7.5 cm) just below a node, and then you can grow a new plant from the cutting. By fall it will have formed a tuber.

Do not plant them outside until the weather has warmed up — usually about two weeks after the last frost date. Pinch off the first flower buds.

THE AUTHOR IN BEGONIA FIELDS IN BELGIUM

Position the plants so that you will be able to enjoy their maximum effect — the bottom leaf of the plant points to the direction the flowers will face! For blooms of maximum size, remove the buds of the smaller single female flowers, which are found on either side of the central bud for the larger male bloom.

Begonias grow best in partial shade. They prefer moist, but not wet, soil rich in leaf mold. Avoid splashing water on the foliage as this promotes mildew and botrytis.

After a season of good growth with adequate fertilization, the tubers will increase in size. After the stem has been allowed to dry and wither, cut it off just above the tuber. Store the washed, dried tubers in peat moss, vermiculite or sand at 45° to 60°F (7° to 15°C). Next spring they can be cut in half as long as each half has at least one tiny pink bud showing. Dust the cut surface with powdered sulfer to promote healing.

Semi-shade   Average to moist   6–18 in (15–45 cm)

(45 to 180 cm), with large leaves that may be green, burgundy or striped. The flowers are red, yellow, orange, pink or bicolored, and should be removed as soon as finished blooming to promote continuous rebloom. Cannas perform best in rich moist soil in full sun, either in the ground or in large containers. They help to produce a lush, tropical effect in your garden.

For best results, start the rhizomes indoors six weeks before the last frost date. The resulting plants can be moved outdoors two weeks after the last frost date. Space them 1 to 2 feet (30 to 60 cm) apart, depending on the predicted mature size. In dry weather, soak them thoroughly and mulch them to retain moisture.

After the first frost, lift the rhizomes and allow them to cure (see p. 75) for several days. Cut off the tops and put the rhizomes in a mesh bag or slatted box so air can circulate. Store them over the winter in a cool place.

| Sun | Average to moist | 1–6 ft (45–180 cm) |

Canna   lilies grow from rhizomes into lush tropical plants with colorful blooms. Much loved by Victorians, they are now enjoying a return to popularity. They range in height from 1 ½ to 6 feet

Crocosmia   (syn. *Montbretia*) grow from corms that are hardy to Zone 7, and perhaps colder areas if they are mulched well with leaves and a cooperative snow cover. Wands of bright red, orange and yellow flowers bloom in late summer from clumps of erect, sword-shaped leaves. They are best in good, well-drained soil.

| Sun | Average | 18–36 in (45–100 cm) |

Dahlias were introduced to cultivation from Mexico over 400 years ago and were named for Andreas Dahl, so they should probably be called *dahl'-ya* instead of the usual *day'-li-ya*. The original single-flowered species have been hybridized into an amazing number of cultivars ranging in height from 1 to 6 feet (30 to 180 cm). They are classified according to height and bloom type — from the large decorative "dinnerplate" types to the cactus or quilled sorts and the balls or pom-poms. The anemone and mignon types are single-flowered with variations. Bronze-leaf cultivars add yet another type of interest.

Dahlias prefer a well-drained clay loam with lots of compost or manure and a thorough weekly watering in a full-sun location. Several new cutting-grown varieties are excellent for use in large containers, including the Baby Dahl series from New Zealand.

They can be grown from seed (only the species come true to variety) or from cuttings taken from young growth before the stems become hollow. Most cultivars are grown from tubers produced from the previous year's plants — even seed and cutting-grown plants produce a clump of tubers at the base of the stem by the end of the growing season. Each tuber produces an eye or bud at the junction where the tuber meets the old stem. The tuber must be carefully cut away to ensure that the bud remains undamaged. A tuber without an eye is blind and will not produce a new plant.

You can start dahlias indoors, or plant the tubers outdoors once the danger of frost is past. The tubers should be placed 6 to 8 inches (15 to 20 cm) deep and covered with 3 inches (7.5 cm) of soil. Add more soil as the new shoot grows.

DAHLIAS WITH BRONZE FOLIAGE

Insert a support stake at planting time to avoid possible damage to the tuber later. If you want bushy plants with lots of bloom rather than a few flowers of exhibition quality, pinch off the tip of the main stem when it is about a foot (30 cm) tall to promote lots of side branches.

After the first killing frost, carefully dig up the plant, shake off the soil and allow to cure (see p.75). When cutting off the stem, leave several inches (centimeters) to allow for easier tuber division. I suggest you store each clump intact, dividing the tubers if desired in the early spring when the buds or eyes are visible. Store in sand, peat or vermiculite at 35° to 50°F (2° to 10°C).

Sun	Average	1–6 ft (30–180 cm)

Eucharis amazonica, known as Amazon lily, has deep green foliage reaching a height of 1 ½ to 2 feet (45 to 60 cm). Each stem produces several fragrant flowers that resemble white daffodils. This bulb is best grown as a pot plant in regular potting soil and kept outdoors in the summer (an excellent addition to your potscaping!) and overwintered as a houseplant. If left undisturbed and maintained at 50° to 60°F (10° to 15°C) during the winter, the foliage will remain green. When it becomes necessary to divide or repot, do it in early spring.

Semi-shade   Average   1–2 ft (45–60 cm)

Eucomis are native to South Africa's eastern Cape, where they grow in the rainy summer and are dormant and dry in the winter. They are a perfect summer bulb for pot culture. Start them indoors six weeks before the last frost date. Plant one bulb per 6- to 8-inch (15 to 20 cm) pot or three per 12- to 14-inch (30 to 35 cm) size. Water them well to trigger the growth of the rosette of decorative foliage. This will be followed by a sturdy flower spike densely packed with almost flat flowers and topped by a tuft of small leaves — hence the name pineapple flower. This flower spike will remain decorative for a long time. *E. bicolor* produces a 1- foot (30 cm) purple blotched flower stem with individual blossoms that are soft green edged with purple. *E. comosa* has a 1 ½-foot (45 cm) stem with pink flowers centered with purple. The pure white flowers of *E. autumnalis* bloom in late summer. The pots can be stored dry in a cool room during the winter.

Sun	Average	1–1 ½ ft (30–45 cm)

Galtonia candicans can become a permanent member of the flower garden for gardeners in Zone 7. For those in colder climates, it makes the perfect center for a large tub. Four to five feet (1.2 to 1.5 m) high, and sometimes described as a summer hyacinth, galtonia requires fertile soil, adequate moisture and full sun. Plant the bulbs 4 inches (10 cm) deep in the garden or start them indoors six weeks before the last frost date. The flower stalk, rising above the long strap-like basal leaves, produces many pendant ivory-white fragrant blossoms.

Sun	Average	4–5 ft (1.2–1.5 m)

Gladiolus byzantinus

Gladiolus has long been popular as a cut flower and in garden borders. *G. nanus, G. colviliei* and related South African species grow 1 ½ to 2 feet (45 to 60 cm) tall and can be hardy to Zone 7. They have fewer flowers per spike than the well-known hybrids. The hybrids are divided into groups according to their height and flower size — the largest growing 5 to 6 feet (1.5 to 1.8 m) tall. The small-flowered miniatures, reaching only 2 to 3 feet (60 to 100 cm), are a better choice for small gardens. Colors cover the whole spectrum and include many bicolors. They should be planted 3 inches (7.5 cm) deep in early spring. If you wish to use them as cut flowers, stagger the planting over four weeks starting four weeks before the last frost date to allow for a succession of blooms.

G. communis subsp. *byzantinus* is hardy to Zone 6 and is offered for sale in the autumn. It grows 2 to 3 feet (60 to 100 cm) and has spikes of reddish-purple flowers in early summer.

Gladiolus corms should be cured, cleaned and treated with an insecticide for thrips before storing them for winter in mesh onion bags, which allow good air circulation. Store them in conditions that are as cool as possible.

| Sun | Average | 1½–6 ft (45–180 cm) |

Haemanthus multiflorus is the perfect easy-care bulb to add fireworks to your summer potscaping. Plant in a 6- to 8-inch (15 to 20 cm) pot six weeks before the last frost date with the bulb's tip level with the surface. It needs temperatures of 60°F (15°C) to start growing. A stout stem of 12 to 18 inches (30 to 45 cm) is topped by a 4- to 6- inch (10 to 15 cm) diameter round umbel of 200 flowers! Each small red bloom has a long protruding stamen — sure to elicit lots of oohs and aahs! The tuft of broad green leaves continues growing after flowering is finished. This bulb can be left in its pot and wintered dry in a cool spot — it likes to be potbound so simply resume watering next spring.

There is a white form, *H. albiflos*, which blooms in late summer. This makes a good houseplant as the leaves stay green during dormancy.

Sun/semi-shade   Average   12–18 in (30–45 cm)

Hedychium, known as ginger lily, range in height from 4 to 7 feet (1.2 to 2 m) and have glossy, lance-shaped leaves (striped varieties are becoming available) and long slender stems with spikes of exotic blooms of yellow, red, white or pink. The rhizomes should be planted indoors in large pots in spring and moved outdoors when the temperature remains above 50°F (10°C) at night. They need lots of water and can even be left standing in water. Keep them almost dry during the winter. The foliage will stay evergreen so this becomes a good solarium plant. Stalks that have flowered should be removed as they will not flower again.

Sun   Moist to wet conditions   4–7 ft (1.2–2 m)

Hymenocallis (syn. *Ismene*), known as spider lily or Peruvian daffodil, is usually available in two types: *Hymenocallis* x *festalis*, with fragrant white flowers and *H.* 'Sulphur Queen', with sweet-smelling primrose yellow blossoms. These bulbs are best grown as pot plants, although the pots can be buried in the garden for effect. Plant each bulb deep in a 6- to 8-inch (15 to 20 cm) pot. They need plenty of water and a regular application of plant food formulated for acid-loving plants. In the autumn, dry and overwinter at 50°F (10°C).

| Sun | Moist to wet conditions | 18–30 in (45–75 cm) |

Nerine bowdenii is a fall-flowering member of the amaryllis family from South Africa that is hardy to Zone 7. Slightly taller than the *Amaryllis belladonna*, nerines should be planted about 6 to 8 inches (15 to 20 cm) apart. In colder areas, it makes a good pot plant, dormant during the summer. For the best effect, plant three bulbs in an 8-inch (20 cm) pot in the spring as soon as the bulbs are available, with the neck of the bulbs just protruding above the soil. The flower stalks will appear in late summer, followed by flowers with narrow pink crinkled petals. Keep it in a sunny window or a solarium over the winter. When the flowering is finished, the leaves begin to grow. They die down in the spring. Let it remain quite dry over the summer. This bulb dislikes being transplanted, and does not respond well to over-fertilization.

| Sun | Average | 18 in (45 cm) |

Ornithogallum thyrsoides

Ornithogallum has both winter-hardy and tender forms. The hardy members of this family are spring-flowering and summer-dormant. The tender members usually flower during the winter but can be persuaded to bloom during the summer if the bulbs remain dormant (by keeping them cool and dry) during the winter.

O. arabicum has broad basal leaves and stems 2–3 feet (60 to 100 cm) high, each topped with a dense flat head of up-facing creamy white 1½- to 2-inch (3.75 to 5 cm) flowers centered with a dark eye.

O. thyrsoides, commonly referred to as chincherinchee, grows 1 to 2 feet (30 to 60 cm) tall and has conical racemes of 1-inch (2.5 cm) white flowers. This plant is sold as a cut flower.

Plant ornithogallum bulbs two weeks before the last frost date, about 3 inches (7.5 cm) deep in fertile, well-drained soil in a sunny location. If you want to grow them in pots, you can plant one bulb in an 8-inch (20 cm) pot, but I prefer to use ornithogallums in large mixed containers, like half-barrels, in combination with many other plants.

| Sun | Average | 1–3 ft (30–100 cm) |

Rhodohypoxis baurii is native to South Africa. This tiny bulb grows only 2 to 4 inches (5 to 10 cm) high, with narrow, hairy leaves and slender stems topped by solitary flat six-petalled flowers 1 inch (2.5 cm) in diameter. They bloom continuously all summer in shades of pink, red and white, making a perfect addition to troughs or scree gardens where abundant summer color is often lacking. They like a warm, well-drained location as long as there is sufficient moisture. Store them dry in a cool place over the winter.

Sun	Average to moist	2–4 in (5–10 cm)

Schizostylis 'Mrs Hagity'

Schizostylis coccinea is an autumn-flowering South African native. In a sunny or partially shady location that does not dry out in the summer, this lovely plant will prove hardy to Zone 7, maybe even Zone 6. The small rhizomes produce stollens, so a few planted not more than 1 inch (2.5 cm) deep can become a sizable patch. The leaves are erect and narrow (almost grass-like) and the spikes of 2-inch (5 cm) flat star-like flowers are available in shades of red, pink and white. It makes a good pot plant as long as the soil does not dry out. Stop watering in late autumn to induce dormancy.

Sun/semi-shade   Average to moist   10–12 in (25–30 cm)

Sparaxis, or harlequin flower, a corm native to South Africa, makes a good addition to a hot, sunny, well-drained rock garden. The flowers are shades of peach, pink or red on wand-like stems. Start them indoors in the spring in small peat pots and after danger of frost is over plunge the pots directly into the garden, incorporating them in mats of creeping thyme or other flat groundcover. Because overwintering indoors is not usually successful, sparaxis is best treated as an annual.

Sun   Average to dry   12–18 in (30–45 cm)

Sprekelia formossisima, known as Jacobean lily, is a Mexican member of the amaryllis family. It produces a basal cluster of narrow strap-shaped leaves, and each stalk bears one large, deep red flower — the upper three petals wide and spreading, the lower three joined to form a pendant lip. Plant one bulb per 5-inch (12 cm) pot with the tip protruding. During the growing season, fertilize regularly with a formulation suitable for acid loving plants. In the autumn, withhold water to encourage dormancy.

Sun   Average   12–18 in (30–45 cm)

Trigidia pavonia, or Mexican shell flow-er, has narrow sword-shaped leaves and large flat flowers in a gaudy mix of bright, hot colors. These bulbs are best started indoors and after danger of frost is over planted in a hot, sunny, well-drained location where they will have a green background. Each blossom lasts only for a day, but they bloom profusely until autumn. The bulbs are rarely worth retaining for a second season. Perhaps because our summers are not long enough or hot enough to allow the bulb to build up a sufficient store of food, the bulbs do not last.

Sun   Average to dry   18–20 in (45–50 cm)

Tulbaghia fragrans   is sometimes referred to as society garlic. This tender bulbous plant comes from South Africa and has soft gray-green or variegated green and white foliage that smells like garlic when crushed. The flower heads have 20 to 30 small, delicately scented lavender-blue blooms. This plant is happy to stay in one pot for several years, spending summers outdoors and wintering in a sunny window.

Sun   Average   12–18 in (30–45 cm)

Vallota speciosa,   also known as Scarborough or George lily, is now included in the genus *Cyrtanthus* – *C. elatus*. This South African native is best grown in a pot, year round, with one bulb per 5-inch (12 cm) pot. The semi-erect leaves are wide and strap-like. The 3- to 4-inch (7.5 to 10 cm) red or pink funnel-shaped blooms are produced on stalks 1 to 2 feet (30 to 60 cm) high. Although the plant needs a winter rest, the foliage remains evergreen and the soil should not be allowed to dry out completely. It would winter happily in a cool, bright room.

Sun   Average   1–2 ft (30–60 cm)

Zantedeschia rehmannii

Zantedeschia, or Calla lily, originally from South Africa, has been the source of many hybrid cultivars. *Z. aethiopica* is the traditional florists' white calla. It is often used as a bog plant or can be potted and placed in a pond standing in up to 12 inches (30 cm) of water. It can also be used like a canna in the flower border as long as the soil doesn't dry out in summer. These tubers are usually offered for sale in the fall — grow them as a houseplant for the winter and transfer outdoors when the weather has warmed. They can be returned indoors to a solarium in the autumn, or allow them to dry and store the dormant tubers at a minimum of 50°F (10°C). Hybrids of *Z. rehman-* *nii* bloom in shades of yellow, pink, red or purple.

Callas can be brought into bloom any time after the bulbs have had a rest period, and so are often sold by florists as late winter blooming plants. If you want summer blooms, start the tubers indoors six weeks before the last frost date and plant them in the garden just after the last frost date. All callas need rich soil and a regular balanced fertilizer if they are to bloom well again the next year.

Sun/semi-shade	Moist to wet conditions	2–3 ft (60–100 cm)

Climbers and Trailers

In nature the group of plants referred to as vines have long weak stems that sprawl on the ground until they find another upright plant or support to help them in their search for sunlight. Their stems twine around the host in either a clockwise or counter-clockwise direction. If you have ever tried to wrap a vine around a support only to have it immediately unwind, it's likely you were winding it in the wrong direction. Some vines have leaves or tendrils that have adapted for clinging. Others simply travel over the ground until they spill over a rock or ledge to find their place in the sun.

Of all the annual or tender perennial vines that are grown outdoors, only the sweet pea, *Lathyrus odoratus*, is a native of temperate regions. All the others are from the tropics and need to be planted outdoors after the last frost. Most prefer a full-sun location. Some container-grown vines, such as the

Thunbergia alata

passion flower, can be moved indoors in autumn to spend the winter in greenhouses, solariums or sunny windows.

The gardener can use these plants in a myriad of ways. They are a quick fix to cover compost piles, an old stump or any eyesore. An enterprising friend realized that her purple-leaf sandcherry had died but did not want to disturb the garden by removing it, so she planted *Mina lobata* at its base. The vines grew up through the bare branches, transforming the dead shrub into an object of beauty. A utilitarian chain-link fence can be covered with morning glories. Just be sure to take the sun's position into account or your neighbor may reap the benefit of the flowers. Edible peas, beans and other flowering vines can transform a teepee of bamboo poles or tree prunings into a child's hideout or a garden centerpiece.

A newly constructed retaining wall loses its utilitarian look quickly when vining or sprawling plants are planted at the top to flow over it. One of the fastest growing plants for this purpose is German ivy, *Senecio mikanioides*. To provide color, plant trailing nasturtiums or *Bidens ferulifolia* among the ivy.

Perennial vines such as clematis take three or more years to reach their mature size — in the interval use annual vines to fill the gaps. A pretty picture was created on a trellis in my garden when a newly planted sweet autumn clematis actually bloomed its first season in conjunction with the velvet purple of the 'Star of Yelta' morning glory.

Container gardeners can also use vines to great advantage. A few pots of *Cobaea scandens* can quickly enclose a wrought iron balcony. A trellis anchored in a large pot and covered with your favorite flowering vine creates a spot of shade or a privacy screen. Wooden or metal ornamental obelisks in a large pot are very much in vogue. They can be planted with one variety or a mixture of vines, but be careful to combine two vines with similar growth habits so one doesn't overgrow the other. Hanging basket chains are not usually decorative unless covered with vines; some of my favorite chain camouflagers are *Solanum jasminoides*, *Thunbergia alata*, and *Asarina*. Some plants, such as passion flower vine, will actually grow up and into the eavestrough and along the rooftop, making a truly anchored hanging basket.

Of course, hanging baskets and other containers depend on those plants that prefer to spill over edges and trail down. For many years we relied on the variegated *Vinca major*, English ivy, trailing lobelia and various forms of wandering jew (*Tradescantia* or *Zebrina pendula*), but recently the choices have multiplied. Try feathery silver lotus, or dark green wedelia with its golden daisy-like blooms, trailing verbena, trailing snapdragons, trailing violas or cascading petunias — the list goes on and on.

Most annual vines are best started indoors from seed, several weeks before the last frost (some take longer) in biodegradable peat pots. Those that have large seed should be soaked overnight in lukewarm water. Do not transfer them to the garden until the soil has warmed. Vines will grow a foot (30 cm) a day in hot weather but will sit and sulk in a cool spring. During the course of the summer, vines tend to lose their lower leaves. To camouflage this, plant some bushy annuals, such as petunias, marigolds or dwarf nicotiana at the base of the vine.

Most of the following vines are not regularly offered as seedlings in garden centers but make

Asarina 'Bride's white'

good do-it-yourself projects to grow from seed. For more information on climbing and trailing vines grown from seed, see chart on p. 116.

Asarina, sometimes called climbing snapdragon, is now classed botanically as *Maurandya*. The seedlings grow slowly at first so the seeds should be started 10 to 12 weeks before the last frost date. Two of my favorites are the delicate-looking 'Bride's White' and the larger flowered pink 'Victoria Falls'. *Asarina* like their heads in the sun and their roots cool, so provide shade by mulching the root zone. Because they are technically perennials, cuttings can be taken in the fall for overwintering.

Scarlet runner beans (*Phaseolus coccineus*) and the purple hyacinth bean (*Dolichos lablab*) both resemble the pole beans that are grown as vegetables. They will scramble up any support — a foot (30 cm) a day in hot weather — quickly making a screen 12 to 15 feet (3.5 to 4.5 m) high. Scarlet runners produce bright red flowers and large green beans, and the purple hyacinth has purple or white blossoms and bright purple pods. Both are edible if they are picked when young and tender.

Cardiospermum halicacabum is grown not for its tiny white starry flowers but for the large papery balls that hold three seeds each. The seeds are black with a white heart-shaped mark: hence the common names of balloon-vine or love-in-a-puff. This vine grows about 10 feet (3 m) by summer's end and has leaves similar to those on a tomato plant. It can be combined on the same trellis with a more floriferous vine to showcase the best of both plants.

Cobaea scandens should be started 10 to 12 weeks before the last frost date, since it needs about four months from seed to blooming. The flower shape provides the common name cup and saucer vine. You may also see it referred to as cathedral bells. The large flowers open green and turn to shades of purple. A white version shows up better against the purple-veined foliage. The vine has long tendrils and climbs easily to a height of 20 feet (6 m).

Eccremocarpus scaber, a tender perennial from South America, also needs to be started 10 to 12 weeks before the last frost date to produce masses of fish-shaped blooms four months later. They range in color from red, orange and yellow to pink. With a twining stem, tendrils, petioles and hooks, it reaches 6 to 10 feet (1.8 to 3m) in one season.

Gloriosa superba 'Rothschildiana'

Gloriosa superba 'Rothschildiana', or glory lily, is one of the few vining bulbous plants. The exotic blooms are produced in the upper leaf axils, each with six wavy-edged, very reflexed petals of red and gold. The stems grow several feet (about a meter) high, attaching themselves to supports by means of tendrils. I often plant one of the long narrow tubers in the middle of a hanging basket where it can use the hangers for support. The tuber should be started indoors 8 to 10 weeks before the last frost date, with a minimum temperature of 55° to 60°F (13° to 15°C).

Ipomoea quamoclit (syn. *Quamoclit coccinea*), or cypress, vine has masses of fragrant, tiny, red star-shaped flowers that are a magnet for hummingbirds. The leaves are also tiny and needle-like, making this a good addition to a mixed container planting rather than standing alone.

Mandevilla x *amoena*

Ipomoea lobata (syn. *Mina lobata*) is a tender perennial vine usually grown as an annual. The leaves are deeply lobed and the tubular flowers are red in bud, orange and yellow when open, and fade to white. If this is too garish for your taste, select 'Citronella', a cultivar with lemon-yellow flowers.

Ipomoea tricolor is the well-known morning glory. This annual climber from Mexico and the Caribbean needs heat and humidity to thrive. The seed should be soaked before planting either indoors, three to four weeks before the last frost date, or directly into the garden just after the last frost date. It is available in shades of blue, red or white. There are also dwarf varieties suitable for hanging baskets, so choose your seed carefully.

Ipomoea alba (syn. *Calonyction aculeatum*) has the appropriate common name of moonflower vine. The huge white sweetly scented blooms open at dusk, so be sure to position it where you sit outdoors on a summer evening or beside an open window or doorway. Seeds are best soaked prior to planting indoors, six to eight weeks before the last frost. Moonflower vine's large leaves can form a dense screen, and it adapts well to growing in a pot.

Lathyrus odoratus, the sweet pea, loves a cool climate (like the edible pea) and will even survive frosts, so you can plant it as early as the ground can be worked. Seeds should be soaked overnight before sowing. Be aware that there are bush varieties that do not have tendrils and cannot climb. To promote continuous bloom, sweet peas must be picked regularly for bouquets or carefully deadheaded to prevent seed production.

Mandevilla x *amoena* (syn. *Mandevilla* x *amabilis*), a twining climber from Brazil, is an excellent candidate for hanging baskets and containers with a trellis or support, achieving a height of 3 to 5 feet (1 to 4.5 m). *M.* 'Alice Dupont' originated at Longwood Gardens in Pennsylvania and has rich pink flowers 4 to 5 inches (10 to 12 cm) across. *M. boliviensis* is a smaller plant suited for hanging baskets. It has shiny green leaves and 3-inch (7.5 cm) white blooms with yellow throats. *M. sanderi* is often sold as *Dipladenia*. The best known cultivar is 'Red Riding Hood' with glossy leaves and 3-inch (7.5 cm) red blooms with yellow throats. It grows 1 to 2 feet (30 to 60 cm) in height and is excellent in hanging baskets. These tropical beauties demand full sun and lots of heat. Overwintering indoors during winter requires a minimum temperature of 60°F (15°C). Keep a lookout for aphids, which seem to love this species.

Manettia luteo-rubra (syn. *Manettia bicolor* or *M. inflata*), Brazilian firecracker, is a native of Paraguay and Uruguay. It climbs to about 12 feet (3.5 m), and has small, tubular flowers, born singly. The flowers are 2 inches (5 cm) long, bright red tipped with yellow, and serve as beacons to hummingbirds, who love them. This vine has instant appeal. It was new to my nursery in the spring of 1998, and it sold out in just one weekend. You can winter it indoors in a greenhouse or solarium, as long as the temperature doesn't fall below 60°F (15°C).

Passiflora, or passion flowers, have the most exotic blooms of any flowering vines. They are

Passiflora

well-suited to container growing, which keeps their rampant habit in check. Germination from seed can be a challenge but stem cuttings taken in early spring root easily. If you are determined to try growing from seed, the seed must be fresh and soaked before planting. Keep the seeds at 68°F (20°C) for 16 hours and 86°F (30°C) for the remaining eight hours of each day until they germinate. Passion vines are susceptible to root rot if the soil becomes waterlogged, so add some extra perlite to your regular potting mix for good drainage. These vigorous vines need annual pruning once established: cut old wood back to the base. Containerized plants require periodic fertilizing, preferably with a mixture high in potash, but if they are planted in the ground, lower fertility is

Manettia luteo-rubra

Rhodochiton atrosanguineus

wide reddish calyx and a blackish-purple corolla. This vine can be propagated from cuttings but is usually grown from seed. Warm humid conditions are needed to get it started indoors.

Solanum jasminoides 'Album' (white potato vine) is a native of Brazil and climbs 18 feet (5.5 m) in the wild; in a container, this height is reduced to between 4 and 6 feet (1.2 and 1.8 m). It bears large clusters of star-shaped white flowers with prominent yellow stamens.

S. jasminoides album variegatum bears identical flowers but the slender green leaves have wide gold margins. The brightness of the foliage makes a wonderful color contrast in mixed plantings. *S. rantonetti*, the blue potato vine, is really more of a shrub (its stems do not twine) that can be trained into a standard or tree form (see page 147). This is often used in show gardens and parks as a small containerized tree with lovely blue flowers.

desirable or the plant will produce all leaves and no flowers. The best known of the passion vines is *P. caerulea* with 3-inch (7.5 cm) intricate blue and white flowers and small bright orange fruit. But many new introductions are becoming available in shades of blue, purple, red, white and yellow. They make excellent indoor-outdoor plants, wintering happily in a greenhouse, solarium or sunny window.

Rhodochiton atrosanguineus, unlike most vines, prefers a place in the shade since it is a native of the dense cool rainforest of southwest Mexico. The stems climb by twisting leaf stalks to 6 feet (1.8 m). If planted at the edge of a hanging basket, they will trail instead. The flowers hang like bells — with a

Solanum jasminoides 'ALBUM'

Thunbergia alata, or black-eyed Susan vine, is a tender perennial, usually grown from seed as an annual, which will twine up basket supports and cover a trellis or chain-link fence. From a package of mixed seed you'll get some white, cream and yellow flowers, but predominantly soft orange blooms with a dark purple eye. When planted near the edge of the basket, it will cascade over and trail down several feet.

T. battiscombei, a semi-climbing perennial from Africa, has large dark green leaves and 2-inch (5 cm) yellow-throated violet-blue flowers on arching stems that will bloom throughout the year. This is very much a tropical plant and does not like temperatures below 60°F (15°C). *T. grandiflora* of India, similarly tropical in its needs, is a large-leafed vine with 3-inch (7.5 cm) tubular sky-blue or white flowers.

Tropaeolum majus is the botanical name for the nasturtium, a garden plant that thrives and flowers

Tropaeolum majus 'MOONLIGHT'

best in poor soil. Don't be kind to this one or you'll get all leaves and few flowers. Many of the available varieties are short bushy or sprawling plants 9 to 15 inches (22.5 to 37.5 cm) in height that will spread into a path or over a wall, but *T. majus* 'Moonlight', one of the climbing varieties, is a creamy yellow vine that scrambled up my rock wall to put its flowers into the sunshine. All parts of this plant are edible: the leaves and flowers have a peppery taste and are high in vitamin C. The flower buds and green seed pods can be used as a substitute for capers. Just be sure that you do not use any pesticide that is not suitable for vegetables on your nasturtiums if you plan to eat them.

Thunbergia battiscombei

Plants that trail or sprawl

Many of the following plants are referred to as vines although they do not have the apparatus to attach themselves to supports. However, they make excellent groundcovers in the garden and edgers in hanging baskets. They also have the ability to weave through other plants, unifying the arrangement. Many of these have been discussed in a previous chapter.

Glechoma hederacea variegata is a glamorous form of creeping Charlie, an invasive perennial! When grown as an annual in hanging baskets, this thug becomes a star performer, trailing down several feet. Other perennials sometimes used as trailers in hanging baskets are *Lysimachia nummularia aurea,* sold under the name of 'Goldilocks', *Lamium maculatum* 'White Nancy' and *Lamiastrum galeobodolon,* referred to as silver nettle vine. I have also used burgundy ajuga to good advantage in a moss basket. The variegated *Sedum lineare* is a good choice for a basket in hot sun.

Helichrysum petiolare

Helichrysum petiolare, long popular in England, is now becoming a standard container plant in North America. It has been given the common name of licorice vine, although it has nothing to do with licorice nor is it a vine! But no one can dispute its justly deserved popularity. It thrives in sun or shade. Actually a tender perennial shrub from South Africa, it has slender stems and soft velvety leaves of pure silver. Mature plants produce clusters of white flowers. When planted in the ground it is quite drought tolerant, but container plantings should never be allowed to dry to the point of wilting. A gold leaf form is called 'Limelight', and a variegated green and silver version is sometimes marketed under the name 'Rondello', It can be allowed to sprawl as it wishes or pruned to promote bushiness. The smaller silver-leaved plant that is commonly called *H. nanum* is correctly *Plecostachys serphyllifolia*. This proves useful where space is limited but you want the same effect.

Ipomoea batatus, or ornamental sweet potato, is an excellent plant for containers and garden edges. It is definitely a heat lover and yes, it does form little "potatoes" underground! It can be used in sun or semi-shade and grows quickly in hot weather. Never put it outdoors until night-time

Ipomoea batatus

temperatures remain above 60°F (15°C). There is a "sweet potato" for every color scheme. *I. batatus* 'Blackie' has burgundy black foliage, which is now a very popular color in many planting schemes. *I. batatus* 'Marguerita' is pure vibrant gold and makes an excellent underplanting to fill up empty space under upright plants in containers or the garden. *I. batatus* 'Pink Frost' has eye-catching pink, white and green foliage.

Plectranthus zuliensis

    Plectranthus are closely related to the coleus family. Gardeners are just beginning to appreciate this versatile plant group. The best known family member is *P. australis*, commonly called Swedish ivy. These tropical trailers or sub-shrubs make excellent additions to summer gardens and containers. *P. madagascariensis* (sometimes called *P. coleoides*) is a pungently scented trailer with green and cream leaves that will spill 1 ½ to 2 ½ feet (45 to 75 cm) over the edge of a basket. It combines well with ivy geraniums, camouflaging their loss of lower leaves as the season progresses. It's often referred to as Miller's Wife.

    P. ortendahlii makes an excellent creeping plant for shady areas. The round pale leaves have white veins and a purple reverse. Its blooms, produced in autumn, are white and lilac pink. Also best in shade is *P. zuliensis*, with avocado-green leaves, purple stems and spikes of blue flowers. The bright foliage

of *P. discolor* 'Green and Gold' enhances a shady corner. *P. hilliardiae* has somber The bright foliage of *P. discolor* 'Green and Gold' enhances a shady corner. Most plectranthus are perfectly suited to a 12-inch (30 cm) in diameter hanging basket, but *P. argentatus* 'Longwood Silver', the family giant, is better planted in a half-barrel, as it grows 4 to 5 feet (1.2 to 1.5 cm) in one season! Its large velvety silver leaves shimmer in the full sun and it revels in summer's heat and humidity.

    Viola hederacea, or Tasmanian violet, is a charming everbloomer with tiny violet blue and white flowers reaching only 2 inches (5 cm) in height. It spreads quickly, rooting at every node. In a hanging basket it will trail several feet (about a meter) over the edge.

Trailers and Sprawlers

Antirrhinum	*Lantana*	*Petunia*
Bidens	*Lobelia*	*Portulaca*
Convolvulus	*Lotus*	*Verbena*
Diascia	*Pelargonium peltatum*	
Fuchsia (trailing types)	(ivy geraniums)	

Flamboyant Foliage

Color in your garden and containers comes not only from flowers but also from leaves, stems and buds. Foliage is becoming so highly regarded that some gardeners are opting for foliage gardens, where leaf form and color give a full season of interest and easy care. A friend of mine decided that her hanging baskets should contain only foliage plants — she was tired of deadheading sticky petunias and fiddly fuchsias. Thanks to the abundance of new plants from which to choose, her containers were beautiful!

Foliage can enhance your garden in many different ways. Variegated green and white foliage provides an excellent contrast to shades of green. Shimmering silver cools down a grouping in the hot sun. Warm gold brightens a shade planting. But the most exciting foliage color is burgundy — it adds body to a pastel planting and it tones down and blends the hot yellow, orange and red groupings

Caladium

that have become so popular. This section deals with plants that are grown primarily for their leaves rather than their flowers.

Caladiums are natives of moist, slightly shaded places in the tropical rainforests of South America. The papery-thin leaves in shades of white, pink, red and green may be large and shaped like a heart or slimmer and strap-shaped. The flower serves no decorative purpose and is best removed so all the plant's energy can be devoted to the luxuriant leaves. The tubers should be started into growth 8 to 12 weeks before the last frost date. They need a minimum of 65°F (18°C) and high humidity. Large tubers can be divided as long as each section has a bud. Dust the cut surfaces with powdered sulfur to prevent rotting. A good effect can be achieved by planting several tubers in one pot or you may prefer to put your started plants directly into the garden. Caladiums should be grown in semi-shade but with enough light to maintain the vibrant colors. They prefer to be kept evenly moist. In the autumn, the leaves begin to die down and water should be reduced. Dormant tubers must be stored at 55° to 60°F (13° to 15°C) and not be allowed to dry out completely. If caladiums are grown in a pot, simply stop watering and store the tubers still in the pot of soil; this will prevent desiccation.

Coleus, or more correctly *Solenostemon scutellarioides*, is a tender perennial native to Malaysia and southeast Asia, closely related to plectranthus. The plant habit may be erect or spreading, with spikes of insignificant pale blue flowers. These are usually removed lest they detract from the beautiful leaves. Colors range from pure gold to pure black with reds and burgundies predominating. Most varieties have bicolored or multicolored

Coleus

foliage, allowing for great combinations in containers or in the garden. Leaf shape may be simple or deeply lobed and dissected, and leaf edges may be smooth, toothed or highly ruffled. Some are diminuitive, while others achieve shrub proportions. Coleus are guaranteed to brighten a shady or semi-shady spot, but some varieties are sun-tolerant. They need regular moisture and should not be allowed to dry to the wilting point.

Coleus are very sensitive to cold temperatures, reacting adversely to anything below 60°F (15°C), so do not place them outside until temperatures have truly warmed. Choose a site protected from wind to prevent damage to the large leaves. Cuttings taken in late summer make excellent houseplants during the winter in a bright sunny window. New roots form readily from any point on the stem, not just at a node. If growth tends to be spindly remove the growing

Oxalis triangularis

One of the few remaining cultivars from the latter half of the 19th century is 'Pineapple Beauty', a burgundy and gold creation first offered for sale in an 1877 catalogue.

Oxalis belongs to a plant family with over 800 species. Some are hardy perennials, others are tender houseplants and some are dreadful weeds. Two tender varieties popularly used in garden and container plants are *O. deppei* and *O. triangularis*. *O. deppei*, sometimes called the good luck plant or iron cross, has green leaves with a burgundy blotch in the center. The flowers, held well above the foliage and achieving a height of 12 inches (30 cm), are coral pink. The tiny bulbs should be dug and stored dry over the winter.

O. triangularis grows from tiny rhizomes that resemble little pine cones. The leaves are a deep purple and the flowers a soft lavender pink. Reaching a height of 6 to 8 inches (15 to 20 cm), this plant does well in sun or shade. Both these oxalis are excellent for growing in pots. Stop watering them in the fall and store dry and cool over the winter to restart in the spring, six weeks before the last frost date.

Strobilanthes dyeranus is gaining in popularity as a summer foliage plant thanks to its striking color. The long narrow leaves (6 by 2 inches/15 by 5 cm) have a dark green upper surface with a pronounced bluish, metallic sheen that does not quite extend to the margins, and a deep purple underside. Young plants add greatly to mixed containers in bright, dappled shade. Don't try keeping this one over the winter. As the plants mature, they become straggly and less colorful. Cuttings root readily at 65° to 70°F (18° to 21°C) so you can always have a bright new crop ready!

tips of each stem to promote the development of side branches. Winter coloration will be less vivid than summer hues.

Although they are most often grown in bush form, the more upright types make excellent standards (plants trained to a tree shape, see page 147): either full (with a 4-foot/1.2 m stem) or half-standard (18 to 24-inch/45 to 60 cm stem).

Coleus was very popular in Victorian and Edwardian England, where it was used in elaborate bedding schemes and as a colorful conservatory plant. It is now enjoying a revival, and seed-grown coleus mixes are being replaced by named varieties grown from cuttings. A national coleus society has just been formed in England. My coleus collection now numbers over 60 varieties.

Fancy-Leaf Pelargoniums

I predict that fancy-leaf pelargoniums (geraniums) are going to become very popular again in the next few years. They were a great favorite in Victorian England. The children's book *Peter Rabbit* by Beatrix Potter was first published over 100 years ago. Look carefully at the picture of Peter knocking the geraniums out of the toolshed and you'll discover they are fancies. The Victorians, with their love of the gaudy and ornate, developed hundreds of these brilliantly foliaged plants. Gardeners were instructed to remove all blossoms lest they detract from the beauty of the leaves.

Some 19th century fancies, with names such as 'Crystal Palace Gem' and 'Skies of Italy', survived the test of time when variegated plants went out of style in the early 20th century. Only green and white varieties are commonly offered for sale today: 'Ben Franklin', with a double melon pink bloom, and 'Wilhelm Langoth', a double cherry red. All others must be obtained from specialty growers and plant societies.

In most respects, fancy-leaved geraniums are cared for in the same way as their green cousins. They prefer warm days, cool nights and average humidity. During the winter indoors, their colors will pale slightly, only to brighten as the sunlight strengthens in late winter and spring. Fourteen-hour days under fluorescents will keep them glowing through the dullest winter.

Outdoors, fancies do best with an eastern exposure and morning sun or a spot that has some shade at midday. Searing summer sun can cause leaf scorch.

For container growing, use a good quality potting soil or soilless mix. As soilless mixes contain no nutrients, regular fertilizing is essential. But resist the temptation to overfertilize; this will alter leaf colors. To attain optimum performance, water geraniums thoroughly when the soil surface feels dry to the touch. Severe drought causes loss of lower leaves, while soggy wet soil encourages root rot.

Fancy-leaved geraniums range from micro-miniatures to plants of shrub-like proportions. Some have upright habits while others, like 'Golden Harry Hieover', tend to sprawl. This wide range of form and color offers up a wealth of uses in the garden or containers.

The bright foliage of fancy-leaved geraniums will enhance your window garden during the winter months even if there's insufficient light to promote flowers. When the plants do bloom, they may appear single or double in all shades of pink or red, but rarely in white or purple. You may enjoy the effect of the blooms or, like the Victorians, remove them.

Some vigorous fancies can be trained as standards or become espalier subjects. The wiry stems of 'French Lace' make it the perfect candidate for these projects. As miniature and dwarf geraniums age, they develop into small woody plants with tree-like shapes. These can easily be shifted to bonsai containers to become even greater treasures.

Fancy-leaved foliage can also be a valuable addition to floral design. I once noted several shimmering gold geranium leaves as the focal point of a prize-winning design in a prestigious flower show.

Fancies make excellent container subjects. Try combining them with other green-leaved and novelty geraniums with the same color blooms.

Stellar Pelargonium 'Mrs. Pat'

Leaf color

The usual leaf color of the geranium is plain green or green with a brown ring, hence the term zonal geranium (botanically *Pelargonium hortorum*). The zone is actually a red pigment that combines with green to show as various shades of brown. Ornamental foliage of zonal geraniums is classified into a number of categories.

GOLD-LEAVED   This type features very light green or yellow-green foliage. The leaves may be plain or have a brown zone or central splotch. Sometimes they also have a contrasting light green or golden butterfly-shaped marking in the leaf center. 'Happy Thought' is the best known of the butterfly geraniums.

SILVER-LEAVED   With silver-leaved types, part of the green leaf is devoid of chlorophyll and shows as cream or white. Some plants also carry a harmless virus called Pelargonium Net Vein Agent that lightens the leaf veins to cream, producing a meshed appearance. 'Wantirna' is a striking example of this type.

TRICOLORS   The most spectacular of the ornamental-leaved geraniums are the tricolors. They appear in four basic colors – red, green, cream (or white) and varying shades of brown – but the overlapping and blending of these shades give rise to a kaleidoscope of colors. Silver tricolors are basically green, white and red, while golden tricolors are shades of gold, red and brown.

STELLARS   A plant called 'Chinese Cactus' appeared in Australia about 1950, featuring semi-circular leaves with V-shaped sections cut from the rounded edge. Ted Both, a noted Australian hybridizer, crossed this plant with zonals, developing a new race of pelargoniums that eventually came to be called stellars. Vancouver hybridizer Ian Gillam has developed several golden-leaved stellars. His 'Vancouver Centennial' is grown by plant lovers around the world.

FINGER FLOWER GROUP   Also in 1950, an unusual pelargonium was discovered growing in a hotel garden in Mexico. It featured deeply lobed, almost ferny-looking leaves and a round flower with symmetrical petals. The late California hybridist Holmes Miller named it 'Finger Flower' and used it to produce two unusual miniatures called 'Playmate' and 'Urchin'. The small group of plants that have derived from 'Finger Flower' are similar to, but should not be confused with, the stellars.

Zonal geraniums are not the only ones with decorative foliage. The ivy-leaved types *P. peltatum*, also boast some fancy-leaved members.

WHITE-MARGINED TYPES   'L'Elegante', the first variegated ivy geranium, appeared in 1868 as the white-edged sport of a green plant. A very recent white-margined cultivar is a sport of 'King of Balcon' called 'Pink Silver Crown'. A new introduction in 1998 was 'Evka', a variegated red-flowered mini-cascading pelargonium.

MARBELED IVIES   A good example of a marbled or mottled ivy is the small 'Sunset Marble' (syn. 'Wood's Surprise'). Every leaf features a different pattern.

NET VEIN IVIES   'Crocodile', a bright pink single brought to the United States from Australia in 1963, was the first net-veined ivy. 'White Mesh' (syn. 'Sussex Lace') features wider white veins.

Most regal geraniums (*P. domesticum*), also referred to as Martha Washingtons, have plain green leaves, but 'Gilda', 'Lovesong' and 'Princess Virginia' feature foliage with cream edging.

Though scented geraniums are grown primarily for their aromatic foliage, some varieties produce especially decorative variegated leaves. The most impressive is the cream and green, lemon-scented 'Prince Rupert Variegated', also known by its more glamorous name 'French Lace'.

Growing Tips for Fancy-Leaved Geraniums (Pelargoniums)

• The miniature gold-leaved and tricolored varieties are the most challenging to grow. You'll find them temperamental if their growing conditions fluctuate widely.

• The root systems of the fancy-leaved geraniums are not as extensive as those of green plants. Never place them in an overly large pot or they may be subject to root rot if over-watered.

• Fancy-leaved geraniums must be propagated from stem cuttings; they will not come true from seed. Stick cuttings into small pots of moist rooting medium and position in a warm, bright location out of direct sunlight.

• Fancy-leaved plants are often unstable and will sport branches unlike the host plant. This may be a new plant or it may be a reversion to one of the host plant's parents. Remove this branch at the point where it grows from the host lest it overpower the desired plant. If you wish to grow the sport, don't give it a new name. Instead, label it "Sport of (name of original plant)."

• Occasionally plants will produce an albino or ghost shoot that's completely devoid of chlorophyll. This should be removed and discarded. Efforts to root it are doomed; it will be unable to survive on its own.

More Fancy Foliage

BURGUNDY FOLIAGE

Alternanthera reineckii

Amaranthus

Atriplex hortensis (orach)

Begonia semper florens (Cocktail Series)

Beta vulgaris 'McGregor's Favourite', 'Bloody Mary' (ornamental beets)

Centradenia grandiflora

Coleus

Canna 'Tropicana'

Canna 'Black Knight'

Dahlias 'Fascination' 'Roxy'

'Ellen Houston'

'Sunshine Susie'

'Bishop of Llandaff'

Fuchsia 'Gartenmeister Bonstedt'

Hibiscus acetocella 'Red Shield'

Ipomoea batatus 'Blackie'

Oxalis triangularis

Perilla frutescens

Pennisetum setaceum 'Rubrum'

Plectranthus 'Majestic Beauty'

Phormium

Ricinus communis (castor oil plant)

Setecreasea purpurea

Strobilanthes

SILVER FOLIAGE

Antirrhinum 'Clownerie White'

Calacephalus brownii

Gazania 'Sonnengold'

Helichrysum nanum

Helichrysum petiolare

Lotus berthelottii and L. *maculatus*

Plectranthus argentatus

Senecio cineraria (dusty miller)

Tradescantia sillimontana

Fancy Foliage continued

VARIEGATED (GREEN AND CREAM/WHITE) FOLIAGE

Abutilon pictum 'Thompsonii'
Abutilon savitzii
Abutilon megapotamicum 'Variegatum'
Aptenia cordifolia variegata
Canna 'Striped Beauty'
Erysimum linifolium 'Variegatum'
Euphorbia marginata
Felicia amelloides 'Variegata'
Fuchsia 'Tom West'
Glechoma hederacea variegata
Helichrysum petiolare 'Variegata'
Hypericum moserianum 'Tricolor'
Impatiens (some New Guinea and rosebud varieties)
Ipomoea batatas 'Pink Frost'

Lantana 'Samantha'
Mentha suaveolens
Osteospermum 'Silver Sparkler'
Plectranthus madagascariensis (Miller's Wife)
Pelargoniums (fancy-leaved types)
Tropaeolum Alaska series
Tulbaghia fragrans 'Variegata'
Wedelia trilobata 'Variegata'
Vinca major

GOLD FOLIAGE

Helichrysum petiolare 'Limelight'
Ipomoea batatas 'Margarita'
Lysimachia congestifolia 'Outback Sunset'
Solanum jasminoides 'Album'
Tolmiea 'Taff's Gold'

FEATHERY FOLIAGE

Anethum graveolens (dill)
Argyranthemum
Bidens ferulifolia
Brachyscome
Dyssodia (Dahlberg daisy)
Lotus berthelotii and *L. maculatus*
Marigold 'Lemon Gem', 'Tangerine Gem'
Verbena tenuisecta 'Imagination'

Perilla frutescens

Pennisetum setaceum 'Rubrum'

Grasses

Ornamental grasses are quickly becoming a popular addition to flower gardens and containers where they provide an interesting contrast to broad-leaved plants. For best effect, group several plants of one variety together. Grasses generally prefer well-drained soil in full sun. They are used effectively in fresh or dried bouquets. Ornamental grasses can be air dried by hanging them upside down in a warm dark airy place.

Many of the grasses are hardy perennials but several of the most decorative are not hardy in areas with cold winters. These must be overwintered in a cool greenhouse or purchased again the next year. The red fountain grass, *Pennisetum setaceum* 'Rubrum' with its arching burgundy-red leaves and fluffy red heads has become a favorite for use in city parks, golf courses and other large displays.

The variegated form of *Arundo donax*, giant reed grass, makes a tropical looking backdrop for a floral display. The golden orange foliage of *Carex buchanii* provides an interesting contrast in both form and colour.

Annual grasses can be sown directly into the garden in early spring but for quicker results, start the seed indoors 6-8 weeks prior to planting out. Don't be tempted to try the mixed seed packages. Better to try a new type of grass each year while retaining some seed of varieties you enjoyed from the previous season. Some grasses may self-seed too vigorously so cut the flower heads before seeds reach maturity.

The following grasses are true annuals.

Agrostis nebulosa 15 in (35 cm)
Avena sterilis 18 in (45 cm)
Bromus macrostachys 20 in (50 cm)
Briza maxima 20 in (50 cm)
Coix lacryma-jobi (Quaking
   Grass) 18 in (45 cm)
Echinochloa crus-galli
   (Hedgehog Grass) 12–48 in
   (30–120 cm)

Eragrostis (several species)
   (Love Grass) 12–48 in
   (30–120 cm)
Hordeum jubatum (Squirrel's
   Tail Grass) 18 in (45 cm)
Lagurus ovatus (Hare's Tail)
   18 in (45 cm)
Pennisetum setaceum (Fountain
   Grass) 2–6 ft (60–200 cm)

Panicum 'Violaceum' 36 in
   (100 cm)
Setaria italica 4–5 ft (1.2–1.4 m)
Sorghum nigrum 5–7 ft (1.4–2.3 m)
Trecholaena rosea 2 ½ ft (70 cm)
Triticum spelta 24 in (60 cm)

Arundo donax variegata

Annuals grown from seed

Imagine this scenario: a blustery winter evening, a big log glowing on the fire, a comfortable chair and a pile of new seed catalogues. Nothing could be more delightful! Each year the seed companies compile lists of plant varieties to tempt us – some are completely new, some are improvements on varieties previously in existence, others are old favorites popular for many years.

The following chart outlines many of the choices available for seed-grown annuals. I would like to highlight just a few plants you may find particularly interesting. Some are familiar plants that have recently developed interesting variations, and some are brand new.

Petunias have changed in the last decade. They used to be divided into grandiflora petunias with large flowers, and multifloras types with smaller ones. There were also double grandifloras and double multifloras. Then came the Fantasy series

AN INSTANT MEADOW GARDEN USING ANNUALS

with much smaller blooms on very compact plants. These are referred to as millifloras. In 1995 *Petunia* 'Purple Wave' started a trend in a different direction: it grew no more than 6 inches (15 cm) tall but spread from 2 to 4 feet (60 to 120 cm). The "wave" has continued with the introduction of pink, rose and lavender cultivars.

The sunflower is another annual that has changed greatly. Twenty years ago sunflowers were tall with one brilliant flower head per stem. Now they range in height from 18 inches (45 cm) to 18 feet (5.5 m), flowers may be single or double and range from 4 to 14 inches (10 to 35 cm) in diameter, color goes from creamy white to lemon yellow, golden yellow to orange and even to deep burgundy. Branched plants produce many flower heads. There are even sterile varieties with no pollen to stain the tablecloth under a vase.

Cerinthe major 'Purpurescens' is the most unusual new annual to appear on the scene in a long time. It grows into a bushy plant about 18 inches (45 cm) tall. The fleshy blue-green leaves are mottled with white, and close to the end of each stem they form closely packed, deep blue bracts ending in small clusters of purple and pink nodding bells. Combined with trailing verbena 'Homestead Purple' and the dusky purple foliage of *Setecreasea purpurea*, cerinthe makes a striking picture!

Ornamental vegetables such as cabbage, kale and Swiss chard have all become popular recently. This year try growing the ornamental beet called 'Bloody Mary'. Its deep burgundy leaves make an incomparable edging plant.

Each year the All-American Selections organization conducts trials across North America of new flowers and vegetables grown from seed. The winners receive the AAS designation. Some of the best AAS winners in the last 15 years are *Salvia coccinea* 'Lady in Red', pansy 'Maxim Marina' with a blue face, pansy 'Padparadja' with flowers of deepest orange, *Rudbeckia hirta* 'Indian Summer', *Zinnia angustifolia* 'Crystal White', *Sanvitalia* 'Mandarin Orange', petunia 'Purple Wave' and Verbena 'Imagination'. Winners of the 1999 AAS Gold Medal Award, which is reserved for a breeding breakthrough, are Zinnia 'Profusion Orange' and 'Profusion Cherry'. The plants make a flower-covered mound 18 inches by 18 inches (45 by 45 cm) with single blooms 2 to 3 inches (5 to 7.5 cm) wide. The foliage is unmarked by foliar diseases such as powdery mildew and bacterial leaf spot. This zinnia flowers all season without needing to be deadheaded as the new plant growth hides the spent blooms.

The following chart of annuals to grow from seed will help you to make selections for your own garden and containers. See page 149 for complete growing from seed instructions.

Botanical and common name	Description	Height	Flower
Abutilon vitifolium syn. *Cornyabuliton vitifolium* Flowering maple	Tender shrub	6–8 ft (2–2.4 m)	Single, 2 in (5 cm) diameter
Ageratum houstonianum, many cultivars Blue puffs, Floss flower	Half-hardy. Low, mat-forming; tall upright form 'Blue Horizon.'	6–8 in (15–20 cm) or 24–36 in (60–90 cm)	Fluffy, like powder puffs
Agrostemma githago Corn cockle, Purple cockle	Erect, half-hardy annual	24–36 in (60–90 cm)	Satiny; 2 in (5 cm) diameter
Amaranthus caudatus; *A. cruentus*; *A. tricolor* Love lies bleeding, Tassel flower, Chenille plant	Half-hardy annual	18–60 in (45–150 cm)	Plumes or trailing rope
Ammi majus Bishop's flower, False Queen Anne's lace	Half-hardy annual	30 in (75 cm)	Lacy heads like Queen Anne's Lace
Ammobium alatum Winged everlasting	Half-hardy annual	12–36 in (30–90 cm)	1–2 in (2.5–5 cm), daisy-like
Anagallis monelli, *A. arvensis* Skylover, Blue pimpernel, Pimpernel, Flaxleaf pimpernel	Sprawling, intermingles well with other plants	4–8 in (10–20 cm)	Small, cup-shaped
Anchusa capensis Summer forget-me-not	Hardy annual	8 in (20 cm)	Clusters of tiny flowers
Antirrhinum majus, many cultivars Snapdragon	Hardy annual	6–39 in (15–100 cm)	"Jawed" blooms loved by children – both single and double forms.
Arctotis hirsuta; *A. venusta* Blue-eyed African daisy, African daisy	Half-hardy annual	24 in (60 cm)	Dark-centered daisy

Ageratum 'Blue Horizon'

COLOR	MOISTURE	SOIL	LIGHT	GERMINATION	COMMENTS
Lavender	Average	Ordinary, well-drained	Full sun	Slow to germinate (1–3 months)	Can be grown in containers. Many hybrids both small and large and in a wide range of colors usually grown from cuttings.
Blue, purple-blue, white	Moist soil, water regularly	Fertile, well-drained	Full sun	Needs light; temp. 75°–80°F (24°–26°C) Start 12 weeks before frost-free date. Pinch back to promote bushiness.	Use short types as edging in borders and containers; deadhead them. Tall types combine well with perennials; no need to deadhead; heat tolerant.
White, pink, purple	Average	Poor, well-drained, light	Full sun or partial shade	Sow seeds directly into garden or in peat pots 4–6 weeks before frost-free date.	Ideal for cottage gardens, wildflower border. Deadhead to prolong flowering. Seeds toxic. Will self-seed.
Dark red, gold, green	Average to drought tolerant	Ordinary, well-drained. Leaf color best in poor soil.	Full sun	Germinates in 1–2 weeks at 68°–70°F (20°–21°C). Start 8–10 weeks before frost-free date.	Grow in large containers. Also useful in flower beds. Good background plant.
White	Average	Ordinary	Full sun	Sow directly into garden, or indoors 6–8 weeks before last frost.	Suitable for a perennial border or cottage garden. Useful in dried or cut flower arrangements.
White with yellow centers	Average	Ordinary. Good in sandy soil.	Full sun or partial shade	Sow indoors 6 weeks before last frost.	Excellent dried flower. May self-seed.
Deep blue, red	Drought resistant	Light, sandy loam	Full sun	Sow indoors 10–12 weeks before last frost.	Groundcover for a rock garden or the front of a border, hanging baskets and containers. A. 'Skylover' grown commercially from cuttings.
Ultramarine blue	Moist but well-drained	Moderately fertile	Full sun	Sow directly in garden or start indoors 6–8 weeks before last frost.	Cut back after flowering for repeat bloom.
White, yellow, purple, pink and red, orange, bronze	Average	Fertile	Full sun or partial shade	Chill seeds 48 hours prior to sowing. Sow 10–12 weeks before planting. Can be planted as early as pansies. Pinch to promote bushiness.	Borders, mass plantings, edging, rock gardens and containers. Good cut flowers. Trailing varieties are propagated commercially from cuttings.
White or orange with blue discs	Drought tolerant	Light, well-drained	Full sun	Sow indoors 6–8 weeks before last frost.	Flowers summer through autumn; prefers cool nights. Blossoms follow the sun and close at night.

BOTANICAL AND COMMON NAME	DESCRIPTION	HEIGHT	FLOWER
Argemone grandiflora, *A. mexicana* Argemony, Mexican poppy, Prickly poppy	Hardy annual	12–36 in (30–90 cm)	2.5–4 in (6–10 cm) like silk crepe
Asarina spp. syn. *Maurandya* spp. *A. antir-rhinifolia*; *A. barclaiana*; *A purpusii*; *A. scandens* Chickabiddy, Climbing snapdragons, Creeping gloxinia	Climber, groundcover	3–10 ft (1–3 m)	Tubular
Asperula orientalis Annual woodruff	Hardy annual	10–15 in (25–38 cm)	Clusters of tiny fragrant flowers
Atriplex hortensis rubra Asiatic mountain spinach, Garden atriplex, Orach, Sea purslane	Erect, tall	48–72 in (120–180 cm)	Insignificant
Begonia x *semperflorens* Fibrous begonia, Bedding begonia, Wax begonia	Neat mounds of waxy leaves – green or bronze – very frost sensitive	6–12 in (15–30 cm)	Small single or double (like rosebuds)
Begonia x *tuberhybrida* Hybrid tuberous begonia	Trailing and erect varieties	12–15 in (30–38 cm)	Single or double 2.5–5 in (6–12 cm) diameter
Bidens aurea Golden goddess, Bit of sunshine	Upright, ferny foliage	24–30 in (60–75 cm)	Single 2.5 in (6 cm) diameter. Daisy-like.
Borago officianalis Borage	Bushy, greenish-gray leaves	18–30 in (45–75 cm)	Small, star-like
Brachyscome iberidifolia Swan River daisy	Bushy, mounded habit	9–12 in (23–30 cm)	Small, daisy-like
Brassica oleracea Ornamental kale, Ornamental cabbage	Grown for display of decorative foliage in autumn	12–18 in (30–45 cm)	Grown for foliage

Asarina

COLOR	MOISTURE	SOIL	LIGHT	GERMINATION	COMMENTS
White, yellow	Drought tolerant	Poor, gritty, light	Full sun	Sow seeds directly into garden at 65°F (18°C) after last frost, or start in peat pots 6 weeks before frost-free date. Dislikes transplanting.	Suitable for dry, sunny banks. Self-seeds. Decorative foliage – gray-green, silver-veined, spiny.
White, rose, purple, blue	Average to dry	Fertile, well-drained, sandy	Full sun or partial shade	Sow 8–10 weeks before frost-free date.	Useful in hanging baskets, planters to grow up a trellis or obelisk. Will trail over rocks or walls.
Pale blue	Very moist. Good near streams.	Ordinary	Shade	Sow directly in soil or start indoors 6–8 weeks before last frost.	One of the few annuals for shady moist places.
Grown for its dark red foliage; tiny purplish flowers	Average to dry	Any soil	Full sun or partial shade	Sow seeds directly into garden in early spring or start indoors 4–6 weeks prior to last frost.	Withstands wind. Self-seeds. Use as temporary hedge or screen. Burgundy foliage makes an excellent color contrast in perennial borders.
White, pink, red, scarlet, bi-colors	Moist soil (not soggy)	Rich	Partial shade	Very challenging. Seed is dust-like. Mix with sand and surface sow at 70°–80°F (21°–26°C) 16 weeks prior to last frost.	Use in mass plantings or containers. May also be propagated from cuttings.
White, yellow, orange, red, pink, bicolors	Moist soil (not soggy)	Rich. For good results add leaf mold.	Partial shade	Challenging. Mix dust-like seeds with sand, surface sow at 70°–80°F (21°–26°C) 20 weeks prior to last frost.	Seedling will try to make a tuber if optimum conditions are not met. Protect from wind or wind-driven rain. See Tender Bulbs p. 74.
Golden yellow	Average to dry	Any soil, drought tolerant	Full sun	Sow seeds directly into garden when ground is warm or start indoors 4–6 weeks prior to last frost-free date. Self-seeds.	Containers, gravel gardens, borders. Performs well in cool or hot weather. Sprawling form of bidens is commercially propagated from cuttings.
Bright blue	Drought tolerant	Well-drained	Full sun or partial shade	Sow seeds directly into garden in spring or start indoors 4–6 weeks prior to last frost-free date.	Self-seeds; culinary herb, edible flowers; good bee plant. Short flower season (3 weeks). Make successive plantings for continuous bloom.
White, yellow, pink, mauve to purple, blue, rose, violet	Average to moist	Fertile, well-drained	Full sun	Sow indoors 6–8 weeks prior to last frost. Pinch seedlings to promote bushiness.	Good to edge borders, window boxes and patio planters. Plant in sheltered site as can be beaten down by heavy rains. Also grown from cuttings.
Off-white or tinged with pink, rose, red or purple	Average	Ordinary	Full sun	Start seeds in June, transplant in late summer. Ornamental cabbage needs light to aid germination; ornamental kale should be covered with soil.	Withstands early frosts.

BOTANICAL AND COMMON NAME	DESCRIPTION	HEIGHT	FLOWER
Browallia speciosa Browallia, Bush violet	Compact, bushy plants	12–15 in (30–38 cm)	2 in (5 cm) bell-shaped
Bupleurum griffithii Thorow-wax	Hardy annual	12–18 in (30–45 cm)	Euphorbia-like umbels with tiny blooms
Calendula officianalis, several cultivars Pot marigold, Calendula	Hardy annual	12–18 in (30–45 cm)	3–5 in (8–12 cm) single or double, daisy-like
Callistephus chinensis, several cultivars Aster, Annual aster, China aster	Half-hardy annual	8–36 in (20–90 cm) depending on cultivar	Single or double chrysanthemum-like
Cardiospermum halicacabum Balloon vine, Love-in-a-puff, Heartseed	Climber	10 ft (3 m)	Insignificant
Catharanthus roseus Vinca rosa, Madagascar periwinkle	Half-hardy annual	6–10 in (15–25 cm)	Single, phlox-like, 1–2 in (5–10 cm)
Celosia cristata, syn. *C. argentea cristata*, *C. argentea plumosa* and various cultivars Cockscomb, Woolflower	Half-hardy annual	6–36 in (15–90 cm)	Feathery plumes or cockscombs
Celosia spicata Wheat celosia	Half-hardy annual	28 in (70 cm)	Stiff tassel-like flowers similar to wheat
Centaurea cyanus Cornflower, Bachelor's button	Dwarf and tall cultivators. Upright, bushy, hardy annual.	12–36 in (30–90 cm)	1.5–3 in (4–8 cm) frilly, ruffled flower
Cerinthe major 'Purpurescens' Honeywort	Tender perennial (Mediterranean native)	12–24 in (30–60 cm)	Small clusters of nodding bells

Cerinthe major
'PURPURESCENS'

Color	Moisture	Soil	Light	Germination	Comments
Blue, white	Average	Fertile, well-drained	Full sun or partial shade	Sow indoors 12 weeks prior to last frost. Do not cover seed as they need light to germinate.	Good for window boxes and hanging baskets.
Yellow-green	Average	Ordinary	Full sun or partial shade	Start indoors 10–12 weeks before last frost.	Good cut flowers.
White to cream and lemon, bright yellow, apricot and orange	Average	Ordinary, well-drained	Full sun or partial shade	Sow seeds directly into garden in spring or autumn or start seed indoors 4–6 weeks before planting. Germinates best in darkness.	Tolerant of cool temperatures. Edible flowers which are also used in cosmetics.
White, yellow, pink, red, lavender and purple	Water in dry periods	Moist, well-drained, fertile	Full sun	Sow indoors 6–8 weeks prior to last frost-free date.	Good cut flower. Mulch to keep soil cool and to preserve moisture. Subject to fusarium wilt. Do not grow in the same place each year.
White; grown for its balloon-like seedpods in autumn	Water in dry periods	Ordinary	Full sun	Sow seeds indoors 4–6 weeks prior to last frost.	Decorative seed pods. Grow on a 5–9 foot (1.5–2.7 m) high trellis. Combine with other larger-flowered vines.
White, pink, lavender	Average to dry	Ordinary, well-drained	Full sun or partial shade	Sow indoors 12 weeks before last frost. Needs darkness to germinate. Don't overwater seedlings.	Excellent alternative to impatiens in hot, dry areas.
Yellow, orange, red, purple. Some cultivars have burgundy foliage.	Drought tolerant	Well-drained, fertile	Full sun	Start seeds indoors 4 weeks prior to last frost, barely covering the seed. Take care when transplanting to not plant too deeply.	Extended necks on the cockscomb types can be prevented by trimming the root ends of transplants when transplanted into flower beds.
Silvery pink	Average to drought tolerant	Ordinary, well-drained	Sun	Sow indoors 8–10 weeks before last frost.	Pinch small plants to promote bushiness. Excellent flower for drying.
Blue, pink, red, maroon, lavender, white, yellow	Average to drought tolerant	Well-drained; do not over-fertilize or grow in rich soil	Full sun	Sow indoors at 60°–65° F (15°–18°C) 4 weeks before planting outside or sow directly into garden in late fall or early spring. Darkness needed.	Good cut flowers. Make successive sowings for continuous bloom.
Purple-blue with cream inside	Average	Ordinary	Full sun or partial shade	Soak seeds overnight. Start 6 weeks prior to last frost.	Loved by bees. Especially good in containers near eye level in combination with other purple and pink flowers. Destined to be very popular.

Cosmos

Botanical and common name	Description	Height	Flower
Clarkia elegans; *C. pulchella* Garland flower; Rocky mountain garland	Half-hardy annual	12–36 in (30–90 cm)	1 in (2.5 cm) single or double blooms in spikes
Cleome spinosa (*C. hasslerana*, *C. pungens*) Cleome, Spider flower	Half-hardy annual	48–60 in (120–150 cm)	Clusters of single flowers with conspicuous stamens 3–4 in (8–10 cm) long
Cobaea scandens Cup and saucer vine, Cathedral bells, Mexican Ivy	Climber	15–25 ft (4.5–7.5m)	
Coleus x hybridus Coleus, Flame nettle, Painted leaves	Tender perennial shrubs	6–24 in (15–60 cm)	Spikes of insignificant blooms
Consolida ambigua syn. *Delphinium ajacis*, several cultivars Larkspur	Erect, slender-stemmed	12–48 in (30–120 cm)	Tall spikes
Convolvulus tricolor Dwarf or bush morning glory	Low-growing, spreading hardy annual	12–16 in (30–40 cm)	1½ in (4 cm) morning glory-type flowers
Coreopsis tinctoria (*C. bicolor*), various cultivars Calliopsis, Coreopsis, Tickseed	Hardy annual	1–3½ ft (30 cm–107 cm)	Daisy-like blooms on wiry stems
Cosmos bipinnatus and *C. sulphureus*, several cultivars Cosmos, Yellow cosmos	Hardy annual	2–5 ft (60–150 cm)	2–6 in (5–15 cm) single or double daisy-like flower
Cuphea ignea Cigar flower	Hardy annual	12 in (30 cm)	Tiny tubular blooms
Cynoglossum amabile Chinese forget-me-not, Hound's tongue	Upright, bushy, hardy annual or biennial	16–24 in (40–60 cm)	¼ in (.5 cm) forget-me-not, fragrant blooms

Color	Moisture	Soil	Light	Germination	Comments
Salmon, pink, mauve, red, white	Average	Well-drained, sandy soil low in nitrogen	Full sun or partial shade	Sow seeds directly into garden in spring. If started indoors they must be kept cool (50°F/10°C).	Grow in borders. Good cut flowers. Thrives in cool temperatures – dislikes heat.
Pink, lavender, white, yellow	Drought tolerant	Any soil, but prefers hot, dry location	Full sun or partial shade	Start seeds 4–6 weeks prior to last frost.	Good temporary hedge, and in mixed borders. Use as specimen plant in large containers. Allow 3 sq. ft (.3 sq. m) per plant.
Greenish purple to violet, white	Average	Ordinary, moist, well-drained	Full sun	Plant soaked seeds on their edge in 3 in (7.5 cm) pots 6–8 weeks before last frost. Acclimatize outdoors after average last frost date.	Grow on a trellis, wall, pergola or strings.
Grown for foliage	Moist soil	Ordinary	Partial shade or partial sun	Sow 6–8 weeks prior to last frost. Do not cover seed. Do not handle by stem when transplanting!	Pinch small plants to promote bushiness. Named varieties grown from cuttings have become popular again as in Victorian times.
Blue, rose, scarlet, salmon and lilac	Water in dry weather	Light, fertile, well-drained	Full sun	Sow seeds directly into garden or start indoors 6–8 weeks before planting. Seeds need darkness to germinate. Use fresh seeds.	May need staking. Grow at back of borders or against a fence. Good for cutting and drying. Grows best in cool climates.
Tricolor blooms – royal blue, yellow and white (also pink form)	Drought tolerant	Poor to moderately fertile	Full sun	Nick seeds and soak overnight before planting to speed germination. Start indoors at 60°–65°F (15°–18°C). Place 2 seeds per peat pot.	Non-climbing, good for planters, hanging baskets as well as rock gardens and borders. Flowers close at night and on hot afternoons.
Yellow, crimson, maroon, mahogany (solid or bicolors)	Drought tolerant	Ordinary to poor, well-drained	Full sun	Sow directly into garden in early spring or start indoors 6–8 weeks before planting outside. Dislikes transplanting.	Good cut flower. Twiggy sticks placed among plants will help support those in windy sites.
White through yellow and orange, red, pink and crimson	Average to drought tolerant	Infertile, well-drained	Full sun	Sow seeds directly into garden or start indoors 4–6 weeks before planting outside. Seedlings transplant easily.	Grow in a border or large pots. Long-lasting cut flowers. *C. bipinnatus* has feathery foliage. *C. sulphureus* has broader leaves.
Fiery red with black and white tip	Average. Keep evenly moist.	Light, well-drained	Sun or light shade	Sow indoors 6 to 8 weeks before last frost. Do not cover seeds. Needs light to germinate.	Excellent in mixed containers. Attracts hummingbirds.
Sky-blue, pink or white	Tolerates moist or dry conditions	Ordinary, well-drained	Full sun or partial shade	Sow in garden as soon as soil can be worked, or start indoors 6 to 8 weeks before planting outdoors. Needs darkness to germinate.	Grow in a mixed or herbaceous border. Deadhead to promote flowering on side branches.

BOTANICAL AND COMMON NAME	DESCRIPTION	HEIGHT	FLOWER
Dahlia, many cultivars Dahlia	Half-hardy, bushy annuals with tuberous roots	6–24 in (15–60 cm), depending on cultivar	Daisy-like
Datura metel, D. inoxia syn. *Brugmansia* Trumpet flower, Angel's trumpet, Downy thorn apple, Brugmansia	Fragrant, large leaves and large flowers	3–5 ft (90–150 cm)	Trumpet-shaped single or double blooms
Dianthus, several cultivars Carnation, Pink, Sweet William	Half-hardy annual	6–24 in (15–60 cm), depending on cultivar	Daisy-like
Dolichos lablab syn. *Lalab purpureus, D. niger, D. purpureus* Hyacinth bean	Climber	6–20 ft (2–6 m)	Cluster of small typical "bean" blossoms
Dorotheanthus bellidiformis syn. *Mesembryauthemum* Ice plant	Half-hardy annual	3–4 in (7.5–10 cm), spreading	1½ in (4 cm), single, daisy-like
Dyssodia tenuiloba syn. *Thymophylla tenuiloba* Dahlberg daisy	Half-hardy annual with feathery foliage	4–6 in (10–15 cm)	1 in (2.5 cm) in diameter. Single daisies.
Eccremocarpus scaber Chilean glory flower	Climber	10–15 ft (3–5m)	Tubular
Erigeron karvinskianus 'Profusion' syn. *E. mucronatus* 'Profusion' Fleabane	Tender perennial treated as annual.	6 in (15 cm)	Tiny daisy
Eschscholzia californica California poppy	Hardy annual	12 in (30 cm)	Cup-shaped single or semi-double
Euphorbia marginata Snow-on-the-mountain, Ghost weed	Hardy annual	18–24 in (45–60 cm)	Insignificant

Datura

COLOR	MOISTURE	SOIL	LIGHT	GERMINATION	COMMENTS
Red, pink, purple, white, yellow	Average	Well-drained, alkaline	Full sun	Start seeds 8 weeks prior to last frost at 75°–80°F (24°–26°C). Transplant when first 2 leaves appear.	Dwarf bedding dahlias are also now propagated by cuttings. The larger named varieties are usually propagated from tubers.
White, yellow, lilac	Drought tolerant	Fertile, well-drained	Full sun and hot weather	Start seeds indoors 12 weeks prior to last frost.	Grow in mixed borders, large containers. Note: All parts of the plant have narcotic properties and can be extremely dangerous.
Red, pink, purple, white	Do not allow to dry out	Well-drained, alkaline	Full sun	Indoors, 8–10 weeks before transplanting. Transplant as soon as ground is workable in spring after careful hardening off.	Good container plant. Some varieties have a spicy fragrance. Frost tolerant. Deadhead to prolong flowering.
Light mauve or purple, followed by purple pods	Average to dry	Ordinary, well-drained	Full sun	Sow seeds in peat pots 4 weeks prior to last frost. Plant outside when soil has warmed – dislikes cold.	Grow in warm, sheltered spot. Provide support.
White, yellow, orange, pink, purple	Drought tolerant	Poor, well-drained	Sun	Sow indoors 8–10 weeks before last frost at 60°–65°F (15°–18°C)	Succulent foliage. Excellent in hot dry rockeries.
Yellow	Drought tolerant	Ordinary, well-drained	Full sun	Sow indoors 6–8 weeks before last frost.	Excellent edging plant. Good in rock gardens and containers. Self-seeds.
Orange-red flowers	Average	Fertile, well-drained	Full sun	Start seeds 6–8 weeks prior to last frost at 55°–65°F (13°–18°C).	Good for growing on trellis or through shrubs.
White, pink with a yellow disk	Average	Fertile, well-drained	Full sun, prefers midday shade	Start indoors 6–8 weeks prior to planting.	Cold-tolerant. Ideal for hanging baskets and containers. Self-seeds.
White, yellow, orange, red, pink	Drought tolerant	Ordinary; prefers sandy, well-drained	Full sun	Start indoors at 55°–60°F (13°–15°C) 6 weeks before planting or sow seeds directly into garden. Not easy to transplant.	Cold tolerant. Self-seeds vigorously. Does best in poor soil.
Mid-green leaves with white veins and margins	Drought tolerant	Light, well-drained	Full sun or partial shade	Sow seeds directly into garden in spring or start indoors 6–8 weeks before planting out.	Good for cut flowers. Stems must be conditioned by dipping in boiling water or searing over a flame. Milky sap can be irritating.

Helianthus 'Prado Red'

Botanical and common name	Description	Height	Flower
Eustoma grandiflorum syn. *Lisianthus russellianus* Prairie gentian	Half-hardy annual	6–12 in (15–30 cm) depending on cultivar	Single or double rose-like buds open to tulip-like blooms
Felicia amelloides, F. bergeriana Kingfisher daisy, Blue marguerite, blue daisy	Hardy annual	8–24 in (20–60 cm)	Small daisy
Fuchsia, many hybrids and cultivars Fuchsia	Tender perennial treated as annual	12–18 in (30–45 cm)	Pendant bell
Gaillardia pulchella Blanket flower, Indian blanket	Upright, bushy, hardy annual	12–14 in (30–35.5 cm)	Double daisy
Gaura lindheimeri White gaura	Perennial. Best treated as annual in cold areas.	3 ft (90 cm)	Swaying stems of small butterfly-like flowers
Gazania ringens (many cultivars) Treasure flower	Half-hardy annual	6–12 in (15–30 cm)	Daisy-like – solid or bicolors
Gilia capitata Queen Anne's thimbles, Blue thimble flower	Hardy annual with feathery foliage	12–24 in (30–60 cm)	2½ in (6 cm) globe-shaped flower heads
Gomphrena globosa Globe amaranth	Half-hardy annual	12–24 in (30–60 cm)	Clover-like
Gypsophila elegans Baby's breath	Hardy annual with airy, graceful habit	9–18 in (22.5–45 cm)	Small, clusters
Helianthus annuus Sunflower	Hardy annual	18 in to 15 ft (45 cm–5 m)	Single or double, range in size from 4–12 in (10–30 cm)

Color	Moisture	Soil	Light	Germination	Comments
Pink, white, blue, and bicolors	Average	Fertile. Dislikes acidic conditions.	Full sun or partial shade	Slow growing. Sow seeds 16 weeks before last frost at 55°–60°F (13°–15°C). Pinch out growing tips to promote bushiness.	Excellent cut flowers.
Blue (also a white form)	Average	Poor to fertile, well-drained	Full sun or partial shade	Chill seeds 3 weeks prior to sowing; Sow seeds 8 weeks before last frost.	Good container plant. Useful in rock gardens and raised beds. Usually propagated commercially by cuttings.
Red, purple, mauve, pink, bicolors	Do not allow to dry out	Fertile, well-drained, moist	Full morning sun, partial shade	Surface sow (needs light to germinate); 14 weeks from seeding to bloom.	Good for hanging baskets, window boxes and containers. Usually propagated by cuttings but recently new seed-grown cultivars have been offered for sale.
Creamy white, yellow, orange, red	Drought tolerant	Poor to ordinary, well-drained	Full sun	Sow indoors 8 to 10 weeks before planting at 75°–80°F (24°–26°C).	Masses of flowers regardless of heat or drought. Deadhead to prolong flowering.
White to pink	Drought tolerant	Well-drained	Full sun	Sow seeds 8 weeks prior to planting.	Graceful plants for a border; excellent in containers. May overwinter in very dry soil.
Yellow, orange, bronze, pink, white	Drought tolerant	Light, sandy, well-drained	Full sun	Sow 10–12 weeks prior to last frost at 60°–65°F (15°–18°C). Needs darkness to germinate.	Drought tolerant. Good in hot, dry locations. Flowers close up at night. Suitable for windy balconies and containers.
Blue, lavender blue	Average to dry	Light, well-drained	Full sun	Sow indoors at 60°–65°F (15–18°C) 4–5 weeks prior to last frost.	Long-lasting cut flowers. Grow in a mixed border. Combines well with perennials.
Purple, rose, red, white	Drought tolerant	Ordinary, well-drained	Full sun	Sow indoors in total darkness 6–8 weeks prior to last frost.	Tolerates hot weather. Does well in dry windy places, on balconies, in containers. Dry flower heads for floral arrangements.
White, pink, rose, carmine	Average	Soil low in nutrients	Full sun	Start seeds 6 weeks before planting.	Suitable for a cutting garden and fresh flower arrangements. Flowers for about 6 weeks. Plan successive sowings for continued bloom.
Cream, yellow, orange, red, burgundy	Average to drought tolerant	Ordinary to poor, well-drained	Full sun	Sow seeds directly into garden after last frost or start in peat pots 3 weeks prior to last frost.	Grow in borders, children's gardens, as windbreak or screen; dwarf varieties in containers. Taller varieties may need staking.

Ipomoea tricolor

Botanical and common name	Description	Height	Flower
Helichrysum bracteatum (syn. *Bracteanthum*) Strawflower, Everlasting flower, Immortelle	Half-hardy annual	15–40 in (40–100 cm)	1½–3 in (4–7.5 cm) diameter. The best known everlasting.
Heliotropium arborescens syn. *H. peruvianum* Common heliotrope, Cherry pie	Tender perennial	12–24 in (30–60 cm)	Broccoli-like heads of small fragrant flowers
Helipterum humboldtianum, *H. manglesii*, *H. roseum grandiflorum*. Acroclinium, sunray everlasting, rhodanthe	Half-hardy annual	12–18 in (30–45 cm)	Single and double papery daisy-like blooms
Iberis umbellata Annual candytuft, Fairy candytuft, Globe candytuft	Hardy annual	6–12 in (15–30 cm)	Clusters of small fragrant blossoms
Impatiens walleriana Impatiens, Busy Lizzie, Patience plant	Bushy, spreading plants. Frost-tender but longlived in a frost-free environment.	6–30 in (15–75 cm)	1–3 in (2.5–7.5 cm) open-faced bloom. Single or double.
Ipomoea alba, syn. *Calonyction aculeatum* Moonflower vine	Climber	10 ft (3 m)	4–5 in (10–12.5 cm) diameter. Fragrant. Opens in late afternoon.
Ipomoea lobata syn. *Mina lobata* Spanish flag	Climber	6–15 ft (1.8–4.5 m)	1 in (2.5 cm) tubular blooms arranged along a stem
Ipomoea quamoclit syn. *Quamoclit coccinea* Cypress vine, Star glory, China creeper	Climber with feathery foliage	6–20 ft (1.8–8 m)	Small tubular bloom
Ipomoea tricolor Morning glory	Climber with heart-shaped leaves	10 ft (3 m)	Small tubular bloom
Kochia scoparia var. *trichophylla* Burning bush, Cypress bush, Fire bush, Mexican fire bush, Red summer cypress	Bushy, compact, globe-shaped, half-hardy annual, feathery foliage.	24–36 in (60–90 cm)	Insignificant

Color	Moisture	Soil	Light	Germination	Comments
White through yellow to red, rose, salmon, purple	Average to drought tolerant	Ordinary	Full sun. Likes hot spots.	Start indoors 6–8 weeks prior to last frost. Surface sow. Needs light to germinate.	Excellent for drying. Flowers retain their color. Some cultivars are propagated commercially from cuttings.
Dark violet, white, heliotrope blue	Water evenly	Fertile, moist, well-drained	Full sun or partial shade	Sow seeds indoors 10–12 weeks prior to last frost.	Colorful and fragrant in borders, window boxes and containers. Some cultivars are propagated commercially from cuttings.
White, yellow, pink, red	Average, dry	Ordinary, well-drained	Full sun	Sow seeds indoors 6 weeks before last frost.	Excellent in fresh or dried bouquets.
Rose, pink, carmine, purple, mauve, white	Average	Poor to ordinary	Full sun or partial shade	Sow seed directly into garden as soon as the soil can be worked or indoors 4–6 weeks prior to planting.	Easy to grow. Flowers from June until frost. Use in borders, rock gardens, containers. Deadhead to prolong bloom.
White, pink, red, purple, violet, orange and bicolors	Average	Rich, moist, light sandy loam	Shade, partial shade	Sow 12 weeks prior to last frost. Do not cover seeds. Needs light to germinate.	Mass plantings, borders, containers. Maximum height is increased by placing plants close together. Also grown commercially from cuttings.
White	Average	Not too rich.	Full sun	Nick seeds and soak overnight in warm water. Start 6–8 weeks prior to last frost.	Excellent as screen. Grow on a trellis, pergola or on strings. Situate where it will be enjoyed in the evening. Over-fertility causes an excess of leaves and few flowers.
Scarlet, changing to yellow, then white	Average to dry	Ordinary	Full sun	Nick the seeds coat and soak for 24 hours in warm water before planting 4–6 weeks prior to last frost.	Excellent as screen. Grow on a trellis, pergola or on strings. Groundcover.
Scarlet, white	Average to dry	Ordinary	Full sun	Soak seeds overnight before planting 4–6 weeks prior to last frost.	Excellent as screen. Grow on a trellis, pergola or on strings. Hummingbird magnet!
Blue, dark red, white	Average to dry	Ordinary; too rich will cause foliage but few flowers	Full sun, afternoon shade	Soak seeds before sowing directly into garden after all danger of frost is over, or start indoors 4 weeks prior to last frost.	Fast-growing annual vines. Good in large containers with support to climb on, or trailing in a hanging basket. Flowers are produced every day in abundance.
Grown for foliage	Average	Ordinary, well-drained	Full sun	Soak seeds for 24 hours before sowing. Leave seeds uncovered. Needs light to germinate. Start 4–6 weeks prior to last frost.	Grow for foliage effect or as a temporary hedge. Use foliage in flower arranging. Self-seeds. Foliage turns red in autumn.

BOTANICAL AND COMMON NAME	DESCRIPTION	HEIGHT	FLOWER
Lathyrus odoratus, many cultivars Sweet pea	Climber, and dwarf bushy non-climbing	18–72 in (45–180 cm)	Fragrant 5-petalled blooms shaped like an old fashioned sun bonnet
Lavatera trimestris Annual rose mallow, Tree mallow	Hardy annual. Shrub-like plants.	20–30 in (50–75 cm)	4-inch (10 cm) flower with satiny sheen. Resembles Hollyhock.
Limnanthes douglasii Meadow foam, Fried eggs, Poached eggs	Upright to spreading, hardy annual	6 in (15 cm)	¾ in (2 cm) 5-petalled open blooms.
Limonium sinuatum Statice, Sea lavender	Half-hardy annual	12–18 inches (30–45 cm)	Clusters of tiny funnel-shaped blooms on stiff stems
Linaria, several species Toadflax	Hardy annual	6–24 in (15–60 cm) depending on species	Tiny, snapdragon-like
Lobelia erinus Border lobelia, Bush lobelia, Trailing lobelia	Half-hardy annual	4–12 in (10–30 cm)	Tiny, tubular
Lobularia maritima Sweet alyssum, Carpet flower	Hardy annual	4 in (10 cm)	Clusters of tiny fragrant blooms
Lunaria annua Honesty, Satin flower, Money plant	Biennial. If started early can be treated as an annual.	36 in (90 cm)	Insignificant (usually grown for seed pods)
Malva sylvestris 'Zebrina' Hollyhock mallow	Perennial grown as annual in cooler climates	3–6 ft (1–3 m)	Large single mallow-like bloom
Matthiola bicornis syn. *M. longipetala* subsp. *bicornis* Night-scented stock	Hardy annual	12–14 in (30–35 cm)	Tiny, insignificant

Malva sylvestris 'ZEBRINA'

Color	Moisture	Soil	Light	Germination	Comments
Red, pink, salmon, white, blue, purple	Keep well-watered. Likes cool, moist roots.	Fertile, moist, well-drained	Full sun or partial shade	Soak seeds overnight in warm water. Start in peat pots. Dislikes transplanting.	Use on fence or trellis. Dwarf varieties do well in containers. Excellent for small gardens. Watch for new heat-resistant varieties. Good cut flower.
Rose, pink, white	Water when dry	Ordinary	Full sun	Soak seeds for 48 hours. Sow directly into garden as soon as the ground is workable. Or start in peat pots 6–8 weeks prior to last frost.	Borders, middle-height hedges, screens. Mixes well with perennials.
Yellow petals with white margins	Do not allow plants to dry out. Prefers moist soil.	Ordinary	Full sun	Sow seeds directly into garden as soon as the soil is dry and warm, or start indoors 4–5 weeks prior to last frost.	Excellent plant for low-lying wet areas of garden. Blooms early in season and continuously through the summer. Self-seeds.
Blue, lavender, rose, white, yellow	Drought tolerant	Sandy, well-drained	Full sun	Start seeds indoors 8 weeks prior to last frost, or sow directly into garden as soon as soil can be worked.	Excellent cut flower, both fresh or dried, for bouquets and floral arrangements. Flower stems come from rosette of leaves so can be planted in front of border.
White, yellow, orange, red, purple, and multicolors	Average to dry	Light, sandy, well-drained	Full sun but prefers cool weather	Sow directly in garden or start in peat pots 4 weeks before last frost.	Use as edging or in rock gardens. Cut back to promote rebloom. May self-seed.
Blue, purple, lilac, wine red, white	Do not allow to dry out	Fertile, moist	Full sun or partial shade	Sow seeds 10–12 weeks prior to last frost.	Trailing forms excellent to edge containers. Compact types are good for edging beds and borders. Shear back halfway to promote rebloom.
Blue, pink, rose, lavender, white, apricot	Keep evenly moist	Any soil	Full sun or partial shade	Sow seeds directly into garden as soon as the soil can be worked or start indoors 4–6 weeks prior to last frost.	Edging plant, rock gardens, between flagstones, containers, hanging baskets. Self-seeds.
White to pale purple	Moist soil	Fertile, well-drained	Full sun or partial shade	Sow seeds directly into garden in early summer if desired as biennial or start indoors 6–8 weeks before planting.	Cottage garden, woodland garden, mixed border. Seed pods are good for drying. Self-seeds.
Striped lavender and purple	Average to dry	Ordinary, well-drained	Full sun, light shade	Sow indoors 6–8 weeks before last frost.	Excellent all-summer color in perennial gardens. Self-seeds.
Pink, mauve, purple	Keep moist	Ordinary, well-drained, neutral to alkaline	Full sun	Sow in garden as soon as soil can be worked or start indoors at 60°F (15°C) 4–6 weeks before last frost.	Plant where its perfume will be appreciated in the evening.

Nicotiana sylvestris

Botanical and common name	Description	Height	Flower
Matthiola incana Common stock, Ten-weeks stock, Column stock, Gilly flower	Hardy annual	10–24 in (25–60 cm)	Fragrant, single and double flower varieties
Melampodium paludosum African zinnia	Half-hardy annual	8–24 in (20–60 cm) depending on cultivar	¾ in (2 cm) daisy
Mimulus x hybridus Monkey flower, Monkey face	Bushy, freely branched perennial grown as an annual	10 in (25 cm)	2 in (5 cm) tubular opening like little faces
Mirabilis jalapa Four-o'clock, Marvel-of-Peru	Tuberous rooted tender perennial grown as an annual and over-wintered as dahlia	24 in (60 cm)	Trumpet-shaped
Molucella laevis Bells of Ireland, Molucca balm, Shellflower, Irish bells	Upright, branching	24 in (60 cm)	Insignificant white but fragrant
Myosotis sylvatica, various cultivars Forget-me-not	Biennial, or treat as half-hardy annual	4–10 in (10–25 cm)	Clusters of blooms
Nemesia strumosa Nemesia	Half-hardy annual	8–12 in (20–30 cm)	Small, open, orchid-like blooms
Nemophila menziesii Baby blue-eyes	Hardy annual. Spreading, trailing.	4–6 in (10–15 cm), trailing to 18 in (45 cm)	1½ in (4 cm) open cup-shaped flowers. Fragrant.
Nicandra physalodes Apple of Peru Shoo-fly plant	Half-hardy annual	3–4 ft (90–120 cm)	1 in (2.5 cm) round flowers followed by papery envelopes enclosing small berries
Nicotiana alata Flowering tobacco, Tobacco flower, Jasmine tobacco	Half-hardy annual	12–36 in (30–90 cm)	Tubular flowers

COLOR	MOISTURE	SOIL	LIGHT	GERMINATION	COMMENTS
White through cream, pink, deep rose, purple	Requires abundant moisture	Moderately rich soil	Full sun or partial shade	Start indoors 6–8 weeks prior to transplanting. The highly desired double flowers are produced by the yellow-green weak-looking seedlings!	Excellent for beds and borders, near decks and patios, containers. Fragrant cutting flower. Easily dried for winter bouquets.
Yellow	Drought tolerant	Ordinary to dry	Full sun	Sow seeds 6 weeks before last frost.	Heat and humidity tolerant. Mound-shaped plant. Good in gardens and containers
Orange, red, yellow with red, maroon or purple spots	Thrives in wet soil. Do not allow to dry out	Ordinary	Shade, partial shade, sun	Sow indoors 8–10 weeks before last frost. Do not cover seed.	Mass plantings, borders, containers, hanging baskets, at edges of ponds or streams.
Pink, yellow, white, and striped bicolors.	Drought tolerant	Well-drained, ordinary to poor	Full sun, heat tolerant	Sow indoors 4–6 weeks prior to last frost.	Blossoms open in the afternoon and remain open until next morning (earlier on dull days). Flowers of different colors bloom on the same plant.
Green bracts form bell-shape	Moderate	Ordinary	Full sun or partial shade	Sow seeds 10–12 weeks before last frost into peat pots. Keep cool 55°F (13°C) and do not cover. Need light to germinate. Slow to germinate.	Good for cutting and drying.
Blue and white or pink and white	Average to moist	Any soil. Tolerates poor soil.	Full sun or partial shade	Sow seeds directly into garden in spring to bloom the following year or start indoors 4–6 weeks before last frost for fall bloom.	Cold tolerant. Self-seeds readily. Remove plants in summer when foliage deteriorates. Scatter seeds for the next year.
White, cream, yellow, orange, red, blue, purple, and bicolors	Average	Fertile, well drained	Full sun or partial shade	Sow indoors 6–8 weeks before last frost at 60°–65°F (15°–18°C).	Excellent bedding plant. Cut back to promote rebloom.
Sky blue with white center	Water regularly. Do not allow to dry out.	Light, well-drained	Full sun or light shade	Start indoors 4–6 weeks before last frost.	Borders, rock gardens, annual groundcover, container plant.
Blue	Average with good drainage	Ordinary	Sun	Sow seeds indoors 8 weeks before last frost.	Good in mixed borders.
Red, rose, lavender, purple, lime, white	Prefers ample moisture but can succeed with less	Any soil	Full sun or partial shade	Start seeds 6–8 weeks before last frost—uncovered. Needs light to germinate.	Heavy, pleasant jasmine-like fragrance in the evening. Flowers profusely. New cultivars are not fragrant (white is more fragrant than others).

Botanical and common name	Description	Height	Flower
Nicotiana sylvestris Flowering tobacco, Tobacco flower, Jasmine tobacco	Half-hardy annual	4–6 ft (120 cm–2m), huge leaves	Produces a fireworks of drooping tubular blooms
Nicotiana langsdorffii Flowering tobacco, Tobacco flower	Half-hardy annual	3–5 ft (90 cm–150 cm)	Drooping sprays of tubular blooms
Nigella damascena Love-in-a-mist, Devil-in-a-bush, Fennel flower	Hardy annual with feathery foliage	18 in (45 cm)	Cornflower-like blossom
Nolana paradoxa Chilean bellflower	Half-hardy annual with almost succulent foliage	10 in (25 cm) creeping plants	2 in (5 cm) petunia-like bloom
Papaver nudicaule Iceland poppy	Hardy biennial	18 in (45 cm)	Cup-shaped blooms 3–5 inches (7.5–12.5 cm) in diameter.
Papaver rhoeas Shirley poppy, Corn poppy	Hardy annual	16–20 in (40–50 cm)	Single open blooms on wiry stems
Papaver somniferum Opium poppy	Hardy annual	2–3 ft (60–100 cm)	Cup-shaped blooms to 7 in (17.5 cm) in diameter.
Pelargonium x *hortorum*, many cultivars Common bedding geranium, Zonal geranium	Tender perennial grown as annual	12–18 in (30–45 cm)	Prominent foliage. Large double flowerheads.
Perilla frutescens 'Crispa' Beef steak plant	Half-hardy annual grown for foliage (used in Japanese cooking)	18–36 in (45–90 cm)	Insignificant
Petunia x *hybrida* Petunia	Half-hardy annual	6–24 in (15–30 cm), depending on type	Single and double funnel-shaped blooms. Blues and purples are fragrant.

Papaver rhoeas

Color	Moisture	Soil	Light	Germination	Comments
White	Prefers ample moisture but can succeed with less	Any soil	Full sun or partial shade	Start seeds 6–8 weeks before last frost – uncovered. Needs light to germinate.	Excellent back of the border plants. Mixes well with tall perennials. Self-seeds.
Lime green with blue interior	Prefers ample moisture but can succeed with less	Any soil	Full sun to light shade	Start seeds 6–8 weeks before last frost. Needs light to germinate.	Combines well with perennials, especially ones with blue flowers.
Blue, rose, pink, purple, mauve, white	Average	Ordinary	Full sun	Sow seeds in peat pots 4–6 weeks before last frost or sow directly in garden as soon as soil is workable.	Good cutting flower. Dried seed pods are excellent for winter bouquets. Self-seeds. Successive sowings will give summer-long color.
Sky-blue with white throat	Moist or dry	Ordinary to poor		Sow seeds indoors 6–8 weeks before last frost at 55° 60°F (13°–15°C)	Use as edging plant in rockeries or containers.
Orange, salmon, yellow, white	Drought tolerant. Water only when dry.	Ordinary, well-drained	Full sun	Sow seeds directly into garden in autumn or early spring or start seed indoors in peat pots 6–8 weeks before last frost.	Make good cut flowers. Sear cut stem ends with flame or boiling water. Flower texture like crepe silk.
White, pink, red, yellow bicolors	Drought tolerant. Water only when dry.	Ordinary, well-drained	Full sun	Sow seeds directly in garden or start in peat pots 4–6 weeks before last frost.	Cottage-style gardens, borders, wild flower meadows. Self-seeds thickly and must be thinned out to prevent crowding.
White, pink, red, mauve-purple	Drought tolerant. Water only when dry.	Ordinary, well-drained	Full sun	Sow seeds directly in garden or start in peat pots 4–6 weeks before last frost.	Ornamental seedheads are excellent for dried arrangements. Self seeds. Flower often blotched with black. *P. somniferum* var. *paeoniflorum* has huge double flowers.
Red, salmon-pink, rose-pink, purple, white	Water thoroughly during dry spells	Ordinary, well-drained (dislikes boggy soil)	Full sun or partial shade	Sow seeds 16 weeks before last frost. Soak seed overnight.	Although all types of pelargoniums can be grown from seed, only F[1] hybrids come true from seed. Most pelargoniums are propagated from stem cuttings.
Grown for foliage. Reddish-purple with a bronze sheen.	Tolerates dry conditions	Ordinary	Sun	Sow seeds directly into garden after last frost or start indoors at 55°–60°F (13°–15°C)	Self-seeds prolifically. *P. frutescens* var. *Nankinensis laciniata* has deeply cut leaves.
White to pink, red, purple, violet-blue and yellow, and bicolors	Water freely	Well-fertilized loam	Full sun or partial shade	Sow seeds 10–12 weeks before last frost. Do not cover. Needs light to germinate.	Borders, mass plantings, containers. Cascading cultivars are excellent in hanging baskets. Blooms from May until frost. Deadhead regularly.

Botanical and common name	Description	Height	Flower
Phacelia campanularia California bluebells	Hardy annual	6–12 in (15–30 cm)	Loose heads of 1 in (2.5 cm) diameter, upturned bells
Phlox drummondii Phlox, Drummond phlox, Texan pride	Compact mounds covered with flowers. Half-hardy annual.	6–8 in (15–20 cm)	Clusters of 1 in (2.5 cm) open-faced blooms
Polygonum capitatum Fleece flower	Tender perennial grown as annual	3–4 in (7.5–10 cm) vigorous trailer	Tiny 3–4 in (7.5–10 cm) dense heads of blooms
Portulaca grandiflora Portulaca, Moss rose, Sun moss	Spreading ground-cover	5 in (12 cm); trailing types 18 in (45 cm)	Single or double rose-like flower. Close at night or on cloudy days.
Reseda odorata Mignonette	Tender perennial grown as annual	12–18 in (30–45 cm)	Spikes of tiny but very fragrant flowers
Rhodochiton atrosanguineus Purple bell vine	Tender perennial vine grown as annual	10 ft (3 m)	Dangling bells – 2½ in (6 cm)
Ricinus communis Castor bean, Castor oil plant	Half-hardy annual	5–6 ft (1.5–1.8 m)	Spike-like clusters. Prickly seed husks.
Rudbeckia hirta Black-eyed Susan, Gloriosa daisy	Short-lived perennial grown as an annual.	24–36 in (60–90 cm)	3–6 in (8–15 cm) single or double daisy-like
Salpiglossis sinuata Painted tongue	Half-hardy annual	24 in (60 cm)	2½ in (6 cm) velvet-textured, trumpet-shaped
Salvia farinacea Mealycup sage	Tender perennial grown as an annual	18–36 in (45–90 cm)	Spikes of small flowers

Rudbeckia hirta

Color	Moisture	Soil	Light	Germination	Comments
Dark blue or white	Average to dry	Fertile, well-drained	Full sun	Sow seeds directly in garden or indoors in peat pots 4–6 weeks before last frost at 60°–65°F (15°–18°C).	Use as edging or in rockeries. Loved by bees.
White, pink, red, scarlet, yellow, lavender	Water during dry spells	Fertile, well-drained	Full sun or partial shade	Sow seeds in peat pots at 60°–65°F (15°–18°C) and cover with black plastic. Germination is erratic depending on color.	Borders, mass plantings, containers, window boxes.
Rose pink	Average	Rich, light, well-drained	Full sun or light shade	Sow seeds indoors 6–8 weeks before last frost.	Use as edging plant, trail over retaining walls, or in containers.
Purple, fuchsia, orange, pink, scarlet, yellow, white	Drought tolerant	Poor, light, sandy	Full sun	Sow indoors 6–8 weeks before last frost. Mix with sand for easier sowing. Do not cover. Needs light to germinate.	Thrives in hot, dry, sunny locations, along a driveway, in a rock garden. Excellent in strawberry jars. Also propagated commercially from cuttings.
Greenish-yellow flowers	Average	Fertile	Partial shade	Sow seeds directly into garden after last frost or start indoors in peat pots 4 weeks before last frost. Do not cover. Needs light to germinate.	Borders and planters. Add to bouquets for fragrance. In Edwardian times, mignonettes were grown as standards in pots.
Purple	Water freely	Fertile, moist, well-drained	Full sun. Needs heat to start blooming.	Needs long season to flower. Best started indoors 12–14 weeks before last frost.	Excellent trailing from hanging baskets or growing up a trellis in a pot.
Reddish brown flowers and leaves	Ample	Rich, well drained	Full sun and lots of heat	Nick seeds and soak overnight before planting in peat pots 6–8 weeks before last frost.	Exotic appearance much used in new tropical style. Seeds are poisonous.
Yellow or gold zoned or banded with brown	Water only in extreme drought	Ordinary to dry	Full sun or partial shade	Sow seeds indoors 6–8 weeks before last frost. Will bloom first year from seed.	Long-lasting cut flowers. Excellent late-season color in flower beds.
Yellow, red, purple, bicolors	Even moisture	Rich, light, well-drained	Full sun or partial shade	Sow indoors 8 weeks before last frost. Do not cover the fine seed but does need darkness. Cover with black plastic.	Performs best in cool temperatures.
Violet-blue flower spikes with gray-blue leaves	Water only in extreme drought	Ordinary, well-drained	Full sun	Start seeds 12 weeks before last frost. Germinate at 65°F (18°C).	Combines beautifully with perennials. Use also as central plant in containers. Excellent for cutting and drying.

Talinum paniculatum

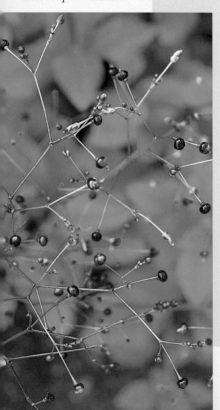

Botanical and common name	Description	Height	Flower
Salvia patens Gentian sage	Tender perennial grown as annual	18–24 in (45–60 cm)	Dramatic large hooded flowers
Salvia splendens Salvia, Scarlet sage	Half-hardy annual	18 in (45 cm)	Spikes of bloom
Salvia viridis syn. *S. horminum*, several cultivars Clary sage	Hardy annual	12–20 in (30–50 cm)	Very tiny with colored bracts
Scabiosa atropurpurea Pincushion flower, Sweet scabious, Mourning bride	Half-hardy annual	18–36 in (45–90 cm)	Pincushion-like flower heads
Schizanthus x *wisetonensis* Butterfly flower, Poor man's orchid, Schizanthus	Half-hardy annual	10–12 in (25–30 cm)	Clusters of 1½ in (4 cm) orchid-like flowers
Senecio cineraria Dusty miller	Tender perennial grown as an annual	8–15 in (20–38 cm)	Insignificant. Grown for foliage.
Tagetes, several varieties Marigold	Half-hardy annual	6–36 in (15–90 cm)	Single or double
Talinum paniculatum Jewels of Opar	Perennial grown as annual	12–24 in (30–60 cm)	Small flowers on wiry stems. Last only one day.
Thunbergia alata Black-eyed Susan vine	Tender perennial grown as half-hardy annual vine	36–60 in (90–150 cm)	Funnel-shaped – 1½ in (4 cm)
Thunbergia grandiflora Blue trumpet vine, Sky vine	Twining climber	15–30 ft (5–10 m)	Tubular

Color	Moisture	Soil	Light	Germination	Comments
Pale blue, bright blue	Water only in extreme drought	Fertile, well-drained	Full sun	Start seeds indoors 12 weeks before last frost. Can also be propagated from cuttings. Plants form tubers that can be over wintered like dahlias.	Mixes well with perennials in flower beds. Also good in containers.
Red, pink, orange, cream, purple	Average	Fertile, well-drained	Full sun or partial shade	Sow indoors 6–8 weeks before last frost. Red-flowering salvias need light to germinate. Do not cover seeds.	Effective used in mass annual plantings.
Pink, purple, blue, white bracts	Average	Light, humus-rich, well-drained	Full sun or partial shade	Sow seeds directly into garden after last frost. For earlier blooms start seeds indoors 6–8 weeks before last frost.	Good cut flower, fresh or dried. Grow in flower beds, meadow plantings and containers. Self-seeds.
Shades of red, pink, lavender, burgundy, white	Average	Fertile, well-drained	Full sun	Sow seeds directly into garden after last frost or start seeds indoors 4–6 weeks before last frost.	Good in borders, mass plantings. Excellent cut flowers.
Pink, crimson, violet, purple, yellow, white	Do not allow to dry out	Rich, moist soil	Full sun or partial shade	Sow seeds 16 weeks before last frost at 60°F (15°C). Do not cover fine seed with soil. Cover with black plastic.	Containers, hanging baskets, garden beds. Prefers cool temperatures. Flowers when pot-bound.
Silver-white foliage	Average to dry	Light, sandy, well-drained	Full sun or partial shade	Sow 8–10 weeks before last frost.	Excellent contrast plant in flower beds and containers. Frost tolerant.
Yellow, orange, gold, red, bicolors	Drought tolerant	Ordinary	Full sun	Sow seeds directly into garden after last frost. For earlier bloom start 6 weeks before last frost.	Use among flowers and vegetables to repel garden pests. *T. signata pumila* syn. *tenuifolia* have ferny foliage and tiny flowers.
Bright pink	Tolerates drought	Light, sandy, well-drained	Full sun	Sow seeds indoors 6–8 weeks before last frost or sow seeds directly into garden.	Use in rock gardens and containers. Self-seeds.
White, orange, yellow with a black eye	Keep soil wet	Fertile soil	Full sun or partial shade	Start indoors 6–8 weeks before last frost.	Hanging baskets, containers, on trellis or fence.
Lavender blue, violet blue, white	Ample moisture	Fertile, well-drained	Full sun	Sow seeds at 61–64°F (16°–18°C) 6–8 weeks before last frost.	Train to climb over an arch, pergola or tree.

Verbena bonariensis

BOTANICAL AND COMMON NAME	DESCRIPTION	HEIGHT	FLOWER
Tithonia rotundifolia Mexican sunflower	Half-hardy annual	2–6 ft (60–180 cm) depending on cultivar	2–3 in (5–7.5 cm) single, dahlia-like
Torenia fournieri Wishbone flower (from wishbone shape of stamen)	Half-hardy annual	6–12 in (15–30 cm)	Small trumpet-shaped flower
Trachelium caeruleum Throatwort	Perennial grown as annual	18–24 in (45–60 cm)	8 in (20 cm) heads of tiny flowers
Tropaeolum majus Nasturtium	Hardy annual. Climbing vines and bushy plant (sometimes variegated).	3–10 ft (1–3 m) for climbers, 9–12 in (23–30 cm) for bushes	Single or double, 2–2½ in (4–6 cm), spur at back of flower
Tropaeolum peregrinum Canary bird vine	Hardy annual vine with 5-lobed leaves	6–10 ft (1.8–3 m)	1–1½ in (2.5–4 cm) uniquely shaped flowers (like little birds)
Tweedia caerulea syn. *Oxypetalum caeruleum* Blue milkweed	Twining half-hardy annual vine.	15–18 in (38–45 cm)	Sprays of small starry flowers
Ursinia anthemoides Dill-leaf ursinia	Half-hardy annual	10–16 in (25–40 cm)	2½ in (6.5 cm) single, daisy-like
Verbena bonariensis Verbena	Tender perennial grown as an annual	To 6 ft (2 m)	Small flowers in flat-topped clusters
Verbena canadensis Rose vervain	Spreading habit, clump forming	8–16 in (20–40 cm)	Clusters of small flowers
Verbena x *hybrida* cultivars Verbena, Vervain	Erect and bushy or spreading and mat-forming	8–15 in (20–38 cm) high, 12–20 in (30–50 cm) across	Clusters of small flowers

Color	Moisture	Soil	Light	Germination	Comments
Orange-red, yellow	Drought tolerant	Fertile, well-drained	Full sun	Sow seeds directly into garden after last frost or start indoors at 55°–60°F (13°–15°C) 8–10 weeks before last frost.	Use for height in mixed border. Good cut flower.
Bi-colored, blue, violet, burgundy, rose, white	Water freely. Do not allow to dry out.	Fertile, moist	Partial shade, shade	Sow seeds 10–12 weeks before last frost. Seeds are tiny. Mix with dry sand.	Shade gardens, low borders, rock gardens, containers. Selected varieties are propagated commercially from cuttings.
Violet blue	Average	Well-drained	Sun	Sow seeds indoors at 55°–60° F (13°–15°C) 10–12 weeks before last frost.	Combines well with perennials, good cut flower.
White, peach, burgundy, red, yellow, orange, salmon.	Water only when soil is dry	Ordinary to poor. Do not fertilize.	Full sun or partial shade	Sow seeds directly into garden after last frost or start seed indoors in peat pots 4–6 weeks before last frost.	Prefers cool temperatures. Borders, rock gardens, edgings, containers, groundcover. Must have lots of room for roots. All parts of plant are edible.
Bright yellow	Average	Ordinary to poor	Full sun or partial shade	Sow seeds in peat pots 4–6 weeks before last frost.	Use to climb trellis or sprawl over eyesores.
Ice-blue dotted sparsely with purple	Ample	Fertile, well-drained	Full sun	Sow indoors 6–8 weeks before last frost.	Unusual flower color. Can be grown in solarium over winter.
Yellow, orange-zoned maroon	Drought tolerant	Light, sandy, well-drained	Sun	Sow seeds indoors 4–6 weeks before last frost.	Good filler in a mixed border. Aromatic foliage.
Lilac-purple	Average	Ordinary, well-drained	Full sun	Sow indoors 10–12 weeks before last frost. Darkness is needed for germination.	Self-seeds. Attracts butterflies and hummingbirds.
Rose-pink	Drought tolerant	Well-drained, ordinary	Full sun	Sow seeds 10–12 weeks before last frost. Darkness is needed for germination.	The most floriferous, easy-care annual for bloom until snow falls.
White, pink, apricot, rose, purple-blue	Drought tolerant	Ordinary, well-drained	Full sun	Sow seeds 10–12 weeks before last frost. Darkness is needed for germination.	Good in borders, for edging, in containers. Susceptible to powdery mildew (do not allow to dry out).

Botanical and common name	Description	Height	Flower
Verbena rigida Vervain	Tender perennial grown as annual	12–24 in (30–60 cm)	Clusters of small flowers
Viola odorata, V. cornuta, V. wittrockiana Pansy, Violet, Johnny-jump-ups	Some are hardy to zone 5. All can be treated as annuals.	8 in (20 cm)	Open flower 1–4 in (2.5–10 cm) in diameter. Some have faces.
Xeranthemum annuum Common immortelle, Paper daisy, Paperflower	Hardy annual with silvery foliage	24–36 in (60–90 cm)	Small, daisy-like
Zinnia angustifolia syn. *Z. linearis* Zinnia	Bushy plant with wiry stems and narrow leaves	12 in (30 cm)	Single, daisy-like
Zinnia elegans, many cultivars Zinnia	Half-hardy annual	8–36 in (20–90 cm)	1–7 in (2.5–18 cm) in diameter. Single or double.

Zinnia angustifolia
'PROFUSION ORANGE'

Color	Moisture	Soil	Light	Germination	Comments
Violet, purple	Drought tolerant	Ordinary, well-drained	Full sun	Sow seed 10–12 weeks before last frost. Darkness is needed for germination.	Use in borders. Mixes well with perennials. Forms tuberous roots that can be overwintered.
Almost black, purple, blue, orange, red, yellow, white	Evenly moist	Fertile	Full sun, partial shade in hot areas	Sow in midwinter for early spring bloom.	Cold tolerant. Can be planted in gardens before last frost. Now being sold for fall planting. Some are fragrant. Many are bicolor.
Rose, pink, lilac, white	Average	Ordinary, sandy	Full sun	Sow seed directly into garden after last frost or indoors 6–8 weeks before last frost.	Ideal for cutting and drying. Mass plantings, meadow gardens.
Orange, white, pink	Drought tolerant	Fertile, well-drained	Full sun, heat tolerant	Sow indoors at 75°F (21°C) 4 weeks before last frost	Flowers are slow to ripen so no need to deadhead. Produces masses of blooms. Good in containers or gardens.
Bright red, rose, pink, coral, orange, gold, yellow, ivory, bicolors	Tolerant of drought and heat	Fertile, well-drained	Full sun	Sow seed directly into garden after last frost or indoors at 75°F (21°C) in peat pots 4 weeks before last frost	Beds and borders. Good cut flowers. Subject to mildew. If necessary to water, don't wet leaves.

Culture and Propagation

Growing Annuals in the Garden

When provided with the right growing conditions, annuals are very easy to care for. Adequate sunshine or shade, the right kind of soil, and the correct amount of moisture should keep your annuals thriving. Soil that is too rich and continually overwatering can lead to problems such as too much foliage and not enough blooms, weak root systems or flopping plants. The best environment for your annuals is well-drained soil that has been enriched with compost and a deep weekly watering. A very general watering practice is to water the plant thoroughly when the soil feels dry to the touch. Annuals in containers must be given regular care, as outlined in the section on the Contained Garden (see page 32).

Deadheading

This ominous word refers to the removal of spent blooms that are not needed to produce seeds. Deadheading keeps the plants looking tidy and flowering profusely. Remember that an annual's purpose in life is to produce seed — if you prevent it from doing this, it will continue to bloom.

This weekly task really should have a more cheerful name, for it is one of my favorite chores. It gives me a chance to get right into the garden and tend to my plants individually. Consider tying a receptacle around your waist to collect the dead flower heads, something similar to the containers used for berry picking. This will leave both hands free, one to grasp the plant stem and the other to hold your secateurs, snips or scissors. When tidying a stalk with many flowers (such as tall snapdragons), snip off just the bloom that is spent and let the others go on blooming.

With most plants, the flower or flower head is at the end of a stalk; the stalk should be removed at its base. Place your opened cutting tool behind the spent bloom and move it down the stalk until stopped by another stem or leaf. Then snip. When you have finished, you should not see any unsightly cut stems (I call them "headless horsemen").

The trick to keeping pansies blooming all summer (aside from providing them with some shade during the hottest part of the day) is to remove all blossoms once a week, leaving only the unopened buds, which will bloom the next day.

The deadheading procedure provides a good opportunity to check for insects that may be causing problems and to admire the webs of garden spiders, who are some of your best friends.

Insect Control

Your aim should be to control, not necessarily to eradicate. A weekly inspection and quick action will prevent little problems from becoming epidemics. There are natural enemies in or near your garden who will help keep your insect population under control: garden spiders, ladybugs, lacewings, praying mantis, toads, frogs and birds.

I adhere to the "squish and stomp" method of insect control, having earned a penny apiece for each tomato hornworm I killed when I was a youngster growing up on a market garden farm. (I assume the pay scale would be higher now.) When a spray is necessary, I opt for insecticidal soap or pyrethrin. Pyrethrin is derived from *Chrysanthemum cinerariifolium* and is quite harmless to humans but kills all insects, so spray in the evening when bees are not foraging. Insecticidal soap is most effective if you can actually give the plant a bath. Make the required solution in a pail and if the plant is small enough, turn it upside down and immerse it thoroughly in the solution. Insecticidal soap can also be used as a spray. When using any insecticide, be sure to follow the instructions exactly.

At transplanting times, cutworms can pose a serious threat by eating through the stems of newly planted seedlings. Cardboard collars placed so they circle the stem of each seedling will protect them. I have never had problems with cutworms and I think gardeners suffer more transplant losses from birds, groundhogs and rabbits.

Slugs and earwigs are both nocturnal feeders who eat leaves and flowers and hide during the day. Earwigs are identified by the pincer-like appendage at their rear end. Slugs are snails without shells who leave silver slime trails on the plants they have visited. Consider employing youngsters to go on a midnight search-and-destroy mission. Alternatively, place traps such as saucers of beer or lengths of hose or rolls of newspaper for the insects to hide in. They can be emptied each morning into a pail of soapy water.

Aphids (greenflies), whiteflies and scales are insects that suck sap from the plant's tissues. Their sticky secretions result in the formation of a black sooty mold that blocks the leaves' breathing pores. The mold should be washed off with insecticidal soap.

Two almost invisible troublemakers are spider mites and thrips. Both cause the foliage to look anemic and speckled. Thrips also feed on blossoms. A severe spider mite infestation will produce tell-tale webbing between the leaves and the stem. Plants afflicted by mites or thrips can be treated with insecticidal soap or pyrethrin.

Outdoors, the damage by insects is usually minimal, but problems arise when plants and cuttings are brought indoors for the winter. When preparing cuttings, always soak them in an insecticidal soap bath for several minutes. Large plants should be cut back before coming indoors: most insects congregate on the lush growing tips.

Fungus gnats, which look like fruit flies, can also be an indoor problem. The larvae of these flies live in moist, peaty types of soil. Their favorite food is decaying vegetation but large populations can destroy tender roots. Use yellow sticky traps to lure the adults to their deaths, hopefully before they lay their eggs. These traps also catch whiteflies and thrips. Owners of greenhouses can buy beneficial insects who will prey on the bad guys.

Diseases

Curing diseases is not possible. Prevention is the answer.

Powdery mildew causes white patches on leaves, especially when the plants are stressed. Some plants are more susceptible than others (zinnias, begonias). Good air circulation will decrease the chances of infection. If you notice some mildew, immediately remove all the affected leaves and spray with a fungicide. Or try this organic spray:

1 teaspoon (5 mL) baking soda

2 pints (1 liter) of water

1 drop of liquid soap

Rust forms reddish-brown pustules on the undersides of leaves. Destroy marked leaves immediately. If the infection returns, destroy the entire plant.

Botrytis or gray mold begins as a gray fuzz on spent blooms and turns them to mush. It also causes brown spots on leaves. Prompt deadheading during damp weather is an important deterrent to this disease. Crowded plantings watered with overhead sprinkling are most at risk.

The most frustrating disease is a soil-borne fungus called root rot, which causes otherwise healthy plants to suddenly wilt and die. Unfortunately, there is nothing you can do but destroy the dead plant and replace the soil in that area before replanting.

Xanthamonas pelargonii is a viral disease specific to pelargoniums (tender geraniums). Plants can carry this virus but still look healthy until they are stressed by temperatures over 85°F (30°C). Signs of this disease are wilted leaves even if the plant is well-watered, and leaves marked with a yellow V-shape. The plant dies quite quickly, but meanwhile the owner has been removing the dead leaves and then moving on to the next plant, inadvertently spreading the virus.

Always wash your hands after touching diseased plants. Disinfect tools and pots in a 10% bleach solution. To prevent contagion through the compost, put a diseased plant or portions of diseased plants in the garbage, not the composter.

Making a standard

Many tender perennials can be trained into tree form. This practice raises their beauty up to eye level and provides a vertical dimension to your potscaping. Most people assume that creating a standard is difficult and takes a long time. Actually, it's quite easy and can be accomplished in a year. The one prerequisite is that you have enough space to keep the finished product in a frost-free location during the winter months.

Although it is possible to transform a plant from a bush shape to a tree shape by cutting away all but one straight stem, you have better results if you start with a new cutting. The following technique may be used for pelargoniums (tender geraniums), fuchsia, coleus, abutilon, lantana, *Solanum rantonetti*, hibiscus and even poinsettia.

1. Start with a tall, straight, rooted cutting. Plant it in a 4-inch (10 cm) pot. Do not allow any side branches to develop. Carefully remove any leaf buds that begin to grow at each node (the point where leaves come from the stem). Leave the original leaf in place to manufacture food for the plant. This is similar to the pruning techniques used for staked tomatoes.

2. Provide the optimum growth conditions required by the particular type of plant so your tree will grow as quickly as possible (for example, coleus survive at 60°F/15°C but thrive at 70°F/20°C). You can start growing your standard in the spring or fall, and keep it indoors or outdoors, wherever the conditions are best .

3. When the roots fill the pot, transfer the plant to a 6-inch (15 cm) pot. Place a bamboo stake upright in the earth alongside the stem and tie them together firmly but gently in several places. Use ties that will not hinder the thickening of the stem (e.g., strips of old pantyhose).

4. As soon as the roots fill the 6-inch (15 cm) pot, transfer the plant to the next size pot, continuing to remove all buds that could become side branches but keeping the leaves in place.

5. Grow until the stem reaches the desired height and then cut off the growing tip.

6. The node beneath the cut will produce two branches. They should be pinched above their first nodes and then you will have four branches. Continue this pinching technique until you have developed a multi-branched head. Leaves along the stem may now be removed. Always promptly remove any buds that develop on the stem below the head.

7. Support the tree with a heavier stake and place the potted plant in a sheltered location in your garden.

8. When you return your tree to its winter location each year, prune it back severely. Remember that you can determine the shape of the head by making each cut just above a bud that is pointing in the desired direction. Do not allow buds to develop into branches that will grow into the center of the head, crossing over each other and ruining the shape.

Propagation

Most garden centers offer the same varieties of seed-grown annuals – pansies, impatiens, begonias, marigolds, petunias, sweet alyssum and a few others that will bloom in small cell packs to tempt shoppers with their bright colors. However, some of the best annuals could never be persuaded to bloom at such a small size, and consequently they are never offered for sale.

If you want to experiment and have fun with annuals, propagate them yourself, either buying seeds from seed catalogues, harvesting them from your own garden, or taking cuttings and overwintering them as small plants. When planning to propagate from plants in your garden, remember that if the parent plant was designated as a hybrid variety, the offspring you raise will not necessarily be the same as the parent – often they bear greater resemblance to the grandparents (rather like people). Cross-pollination by insects can also add surprises to your endeavors.

Each year millions of seeds are sown by eager novices. Most germinate well but never survive to be planted in the garden. Straggly, pale little seedlings compare poorly to the stocky, dark green plants grown by the professionals.

If you follow the steps outlined in this section, you can produce healthy, strong new plants.

Obtaining Seeds

Seed catalogues begin arriving with the Christmas cards in December (see the source list). Soon after, seed racks appear in garden centers, hardware stores and grocery stores in January. Various horticultural societies organize seed exchanges and everyone feels a little better – spring is on its way!

A seed packet often contains far more seed than you need. If you can't bear to throw out seedlings, learn to sow only what you'll need or can share with friends. Most seeds will keep well until next year if they are stored cool and dry (it isn't necessary to freeze them). Or you and your gardening friends can order seeds as a group and then divide them among participating members. Consider having a seedling exchange.

Collecting Seeds

If you have plants in your garden that you wish to grow again next year, choose a particularly healthy specimen and instead of deadheading the blossoms, allow the plant to make seeds. After the petals drop, the seed-bearing portion of the plant begins to thicken and will gradually turn brown as it ripens. Pick the seed pods on a dry warm day and store them in a labeled paper bag. Some plants disperse their seeds by an exploding seed pod (pansies) and it's easy to miss them. Such seeds can be collected before they are completely ripe; you can finish the ripening process by putting the seeds in a paper bag. Store all the bags of seed in a warm, dry, dark room with good air circulation. If further drying is needed, provide extra air circulation by putting up a clothesline and pegging each bag to it.

You may clean the seed at your leisure on a dreary November day or a wintry evening. You can often smell summer when you open the bags. This is another good time for gardening friends to gather around a table to share seeds and tales of gardening successes and disappointments.

Shake each bag vigorously to remove the seeds

from the seed capsule. Poppies release their seeds very easily, but some seeds can prove to be a challenge. Rolling a rolling pin over the bag sometimes works well. Separating the seed from the chaff may require old-fashioned threshing and winnowing techniques. Using a large bowl, toss everything into the air until the seeds and chaff are separated. Sieves of various mesh sizes that will allow the seeds to fall through can also be helpful. Fluffy parachutes, which tend to fly all over the place when you try to sow them, should be removed from seeds by hand-picking. Place the cleaned seeds in labeled envelopes and store in a dry, cool place.

Before You Start Planting

Most novices experience difficulties because they start seeds too early using inadequate facilities. Only tender geraniums, pansies and begonias are winter projects — the remainder are best sown in early spring. Instructions often read "all you need is a sunny window" but the sun does not always cooperate! I am not suggesting that you have to invest in a greenhouse, but I would highly recommend a fluorescent light arrangement. This could be as simple as a set of lights hung on chains over a table, or as fancy as a three-tiered stand complete with an automatic timer to regulate the lights. To grow seedlings, you need only the inexpensive, cool white fluorescent tubes; the more expensive, wide-spectrum "grow" lights are necessary only for growing flowering plants or raising vegetables to maturity. Set up your lights in a room where the night temperature can be set for 50° to 60°F (10° to 15°C) and a small fan can circulate the air without blowing directly onto the seedlings.

Read all the instructions on the package (unfortunately, sometimes there are very few) or check in your resource books, noting especially when to start the seeds. This is usually given as the number of weeks prior to the last frost-free date. For example, if the instructions say eight weeks before the last frost, and that date is May 24 in your area, begin the seeds about March 24. Make a list of the seeds you want to grow and the recommended starting dates. If you can't locate this information, six to eight weeks is a pretty safe time. Be prepared to keep careful records that include the variety of seed, where it was obtained, when it was started, what method was used, your results and recommendations for next year. Perhaps next season you won't need to plant your seeds so early.

Requirements for germination vary. All seeds need moisture but some like it warm, 70° to 80°F (20° to 26°C) and others prefer cooler temperatures, 60° to 65°F (15 to 18°C). Some don't want to be covered with soil because they need light to sprout (lobelia, salvia), others must have darkness (verbena, phlox) and need not only soil cover but also a black plastic sheet to block any light.

Some seeds (morning glories, sweet peas) have such a hard seedcoat that they should be soaked overnight in lukewarm water to soften the covering. Nicking the seed with a knife or rubbing it with a file is called scarification and is sometimes necessary to allow water inside the covering. Some (snapdragons) require stratification or pre-chilling — this means a period of cold temperature to break dormancy. After sowing, you need to place the pots or flats in the refrigerator or outdoors in a cold frame for the required time — from several days to several weeks. Then you return them to the desired warmer temperature and wait for germination.

You can purchase seed-starting kits that include a flat tray fitted with a clear plastic hood and plastic packs to hold the seeds, or you can assemble your own recycled items: pots and trays kept from last year's gardening, plastic domed muffin or cake packaging, 2-inch (5 cm) deep aluminum pans, or styrofoam cups with holes punched for drainage.

Reused items should be disinfected with a 1-to-10-parts bleach and water solution. Any container that is to hold soil must have drainage holes. You'll need labels and a waterproof pen or a soft lead pencil for labeling, and a soilless mix that is specifically formulated for growing seeds. This sterilized medium eliminates any chance of soil diseases that could be certain death to seedlings. When you have assembled the ingredients, you are ready to start.

Planting the Seeds

1. Fill containers loosely with moist soilless mix and level off with a knife (like measuring flour for baking!). Gently pat down the surface, being especially careful not to leave holes at the corners.

2. Scatter the seeds on the surface, spacing them as evenly as possible. You can use a seeder (which dispenses the seeds individually), a spoon or simply a piece of paper shaped to form a funnel. Experienced seeders often simply spread the seeds directly from the package. If the seeds are very small (lobelia), you will probably be more successful if you mix them with fine sand or sugar and spread the mixture evenly. (Begonia seed is a reddish dust – whatever you do – don't sneeze!) Larger seeds that have been soaked may be sticky and need to be picked up and placed with a pair of tweezers.

3. Unless indicated otherwise, cover the seeds

with more mix – approximately three times the thickness of the seed. Some gardeners prefer to use a fine grade of vermiculite (which is beige) so they can see that all the surface is covered. Pat down gently. If you are seeding perennials that take a long time to germinate, you can use a granular substance like chicken grit or turface, which will discourage the growth of algae.

4. Label with the variety and date.

5. Water by sub-irrigation: place the seeded containers into a tray holding about an inch (2.5 cm) of water. In one hour they will have absorbed as much water as necessary.

6. To keep the moisture constant until germination takes place, cover with a plastic hood, plastic wrap or place inside a plastic bag.

7. Unless cool germinating temperatures are needed, place the seeded containers in a warm place – on top of the refrigerator, near a hot-air outlet or on top of a fluorescent light fixture. If you are very serious about growing from seed, make a propagating table by burying electric heating cables in sand on a table top (the cables are available at specialty garden shops). Remember that when the instructions say 70° to 75°F (20° to 24°C), they are referring to the temperature of the soil, not the air.

8. After two or three days, begin checking for germination twice a day. As soon as the first sprouts are just visible, remove the plastic cover. This is very important – if you leave them under the plastic, you will have spindly sprouts!

9. Seedlings must be grown in a cool, bright location. If you have only a windowsill (south, east or west), turn the containers daily to keep them from leaning toward the light. The preferred method is under fluorescent lights for 12 to 16 hours each day, with the top of the seedlings 2 to 4 inches (5 to 10 cm) below the light

source. Keep the growing area cool; night-time temperatures should be 50° to 60°F (10° to 15°C). Water as necessary by the sub-irrigation method or with a watering can with a fine sprinkler head. Seedlings should be kept evenly moist and never allowed to be soggy or reach the wilting point. A fungal disease called "damping off" causes stems of seedlings to collapse at soil level and then fall over. Use a fungicide as a preventative, following label instructions carefully. If seedlings are crowded, mildew or mold may result. As soon as you see this, remove the affected seedlings and transplant the remainder into individual containers.

10. The first "seedling leaves" do not resemble the "true leaves," which are produced next. When there are two sets of true leaves, it's time to transplant the seedlings into individual small pots filled with the same soilless mix used for seeding.

11. Grasp a seedling by a leaf (even the slightest pressure on the stem can cause permanent damage) and using a pointed tool called a dibbler (or a pencil or popsicle stick), dig under the seedling, lifting it up. While grasping the leaf with thumb and forefinger and supporting the roots with the other three fingers, make an appropriate hole in the new pot with the dibbler and ease the seedling in. Unless the seedling has already begun to form a rosette or crown, it can be planted deeper than it was growing in the seed flat. Firm the soil gently around the stem so that it stands up straight. An application of transplant fertilizer diluted to half strength will hasten the development of roots.

12. The small plants should be grown as the seedlings were: 12 to 16 hours of light and cool night temperatures. Water when the soil approaches dryness. Fertilize weekly with a quarter strength 20-20-20 liquid fertilizer.

13. When the plants are 2 to 3 inches (5 to 7.5 cm) tall, pinch off the growing tip to promote the development of side branches.

Conditioning to the Outdoors

You next need to get your seedlings acclimatized to the outdoors. This procedure is often referred to as "hardening off". A week before you want to plant the seedlings outdoors, you must gradually accustom your transplants to the outside environment. This move can be disastrous — just one hour of hot sunshine on the first day can burn the tender foliage. Preferably your seedlings should be moved out on a warm but cloudy day or at least set in full shade and protected from the wind. Each day give them a little more sun. Watch their moisture content carefully, because they will dry out more quickly outdoors. It is often recommended that they be moved back into the house at night. I prefer to put them into an unheated garage or cover them with a cardboard box or floating row covers (a muslin-like material sold by garden supply companies). Moving them back indoors where the night-time temperature may be warmer than the daytime temperature outdoors simply confuses the plant. A cold frame or small plastic tent could be very useful at hardening-off time.

Transplanting into the Garden

The big day finally arrives — hopefully it is a cloudy one, or you choose to plant in the evening. The garden soil is moist, as are the waiting transplants. Make a hole and fill it with water. When it has soaked away, remove the plant from the pot and spread open the root ball. Place it into the moistened hole and firm the soil around the stem. Mist new plantings lightly for several days until they have recovered from the shock. The addition of a mulch to cover the soil will conserve moisture, keep the soil cool and prevent weed growth. During the summer months mulched plants will need only one thorough watering per week.

Direct-Seeding

In seed catalogues you will often see the notation "direct-seed where they are to flower – dislikes transplanting." Actually, I have never found this to work very well in my garden, which is full of spring bulbs without any empty spaces for seeding annuals. Direct-seeding can be very unpredictable: a severely hot dry day can shrivel germinating seedlings or a heavy rain can wash them away. However, it can work if you are planting a cutting garden and plant the seeds in rows like vegetables. Another successful method is to cut round plastic containers (margarine, yogurt, etc.) into plastic circles, about 2 inches (5 cm) deep. Sink these rings into the ground, leaving about ½ inch (12 mm) above the surface. Plant several seeds within each circle. Once the seedlings are growing well, remove the protective plastic circles.

I prefer to direct seed into small biodegradable peat pots or peat pellets (these look like flat cookies until you add water and they puff up like muffins). The plants can achieve a reasonable size before pot and all are planted into the garden without disturbing the roots.

Plant two or three seeds per pot. If they all germinate, remove the two weakest at the soil line with a pair of scissors. Use the same hardening-off methods described above. When transferring them to the garden, be sure the peat pot is com-

pletely wet so it will break down quickly in the soil. Tear off the top half-inch (12 mm) of the pot so it doesn't act like a wick, drawing moisture from the soil ball. If the roots have not yet penetrated the base of the pot, pull the bottom off too, so the roots can quickly grow down into the earth. Mulch and water as you would other transplants.

Growing from Stem Cuttings

Some annuals and most tender perennials can be propagated by stem cuttings. If you have sunny windows, a solarium or a fluorescent light set-up, this is an excellent way to retain certain plants and to increase their numbers if so desired for the next year's season.

Unfortunately, many people wait until the weather forecaster predicts frost and they then rush out, snip some cuttings and put them in a jar of water. The success rate of this method is often limited. Roots that grow in water have a different structure than those in soil and when you pot the plants into soil they must make new roots. The better way is to take cuttings in late summer before night temperatures have plunged. Start the cuttings directly in the same type of soilless mix that you use for starting seeds in small 2 ½ inch (6.25 cm) pots or recycled plastic containers. Some gardeners prefer to use vermiculite or a half-peat moss and half-perlite mix.

Take cuttings from vigorous, healthy plants, preferably choosing non-flowering shoots. Using a sharp knife, make a cut just above a node about 4 inches (10 cm) from the tip. Then prepare the cutting by removing all but one fully expanded leaf and the terminal bud. Remove any flower buds. Make a fresh, straight cut just below the bottom node. Insert the prepared cutting into a small clean pot of moist mix. Providing heat from below and constant humidity will promote quick rooting (just as they encourage seed germination). The top of the refrigerator is a good place. Keep the cuttings out of direct sunlight to prevent wilting. Cover them with some kind of plastic humidity hood, at least until they have recovered from the shock of being cut. Roots will form in one to three weeks. When they resist a gentle tug their roots have formed. When roots are in place, grow the plants in a bright cool location (like seedlings), either in your sunniest window or on a fluorescent light stand with the top of the plant 4 to 6 inches (10 to 15 cm) below the light fixture. Transplant to the next size pot when the roots fill the starter pot. Other signs that a plant is ready for a bigger pot are when it dries out very quickly after watering and when it becomes top heavy and keeps falling over. As the plant outgrows each pot, keep transplanting to a pot one size larger until you are ready to plant

them outside. Fertilize regularly as long as the plant is actively growing. I prefer a weekly quarter-strength application of 20-20-20 rather than a monthly feeding. Pinch off the growing tip to promote bushiness or wait until the plant is about 6 inches (15 cm) tall and remove the top 2 ½ to 3 inches (6.25 to 7.5 cm) for another cutting (this is what the professionals do). The new plants will need a hardening-off period and should be planted in the same way you plant any other seedling.

Frost dates

To find out what the last frost and the first frost dates are in your area, contact your local Extension Agent (United States) or your local Agricultural Office (Canada).

Botanical Language

Common names for plants vary from one region to another – even sometimes from one garden to another! To correctly identify plants, it is essential to use Latin nomenclature. In the text, common names have been included in parentheses where it's been possible to do so.

Here are some examples to help beginners understand the Latin system of botanical names.

Lavatera trimestris 'Mont Blanc'
Lavatera is the genus; *trimestris*, the species; and 'Mont Blanc', the cultivar. The words "variety" and "cultivar" are often used interchangeably. However, technically a variety is a plant that differs in some way from the true species (perhaps with variegated foliage or a different color of flower) while a cultivar (from the term "cultivated variety") is developed by a plant breeder by deliberately cross-pollinating two plants.

Pelargonium **x** *hortorum* 'Maverick Star'
When two different species are cross-pollinated, the Latin name will include "**x**". In this example the genus is *Pelargonium*. The species is *hortorum*, and the "**x**" signifies that this is a cross between two different species (in this case *P. inquinans* **x** *P. zonale*). The cultivar 'Maverick Star' is an F1 hybrid, a new plant that results from the cross-pollination of two plants with different genetic traits. Seeds from this new plant will not come true (that is, they will not produce plants with the same qualities as the plant that produced the seed). Cross-pollination is a labor-intensive process that must be repeated for each seed production. F1 hybrid seeds are noted for their vigor; quickness to flower; uniformity of habit, color, and size; resistance to disease; and, of course, greater cost.

Eustoma grandiflorum syn. *Lisianthus*
You will often see the abbreviation "syn". This is short for "synonym". In this example, it means that botanists have recently changed the name from *Lisianthus* to *Eustoma*.

Selected sources of annuals

Following is a list of recommended nurseries and seed houses. We have indicated where there is a charge for a catalogue:

In the United States of America

Alannah's African Violets
  (pelargoniums)
3159 Hwy 21 North
Box 10101
Danville, WA 99121
www.alannahs.com
Wide variety of geraniums.
On-line catalog.

Glasshouse Works (plants)
P.O. Box 97, Church Street
Stewart, OH 45778-0097
Info (740) 662-2142
Orders Toll-Free 800-837-2142
Fax (740) 662-2120
www.glasshouseworks.com
On-line catalogue.

Heronswood Nursery (plants)
7530 NE 288th Street
Kingston, WA 98346-9502
(360) 297-4172
Fax (360) 297-8321
www.heronswood.com
Send $8 for catalogue.

Logee's Greenhouses (plants)
141 North Street
Danielson, CT 06239-1939
(860) 774-8038
Toll-Free 888-330-8038
Fax (860) 774-9932
Fax Toll-Free 888-774-9932
www.logees.com
Send $3 for catalogue.

Park Seed Co. Inc. (plants)
1 Parkton Avenue
Greenwood, SC 29647-0001
Toll-Free 800-845-3369
Fax Toll-Free 800-941-4206
www.parkseed.com
One of the country's largest seed houses;
  authorized to sell Outback Plants®.
  On-line catalogue.

Plant Delights Nursery (plants)
9241 Sauls Road
Raleigh, NC 27603-9326
(919) 772-4794
Fax (919) 662-0370
www.plantdel.com
For catalogue send 10 first-class US postage
  stamps or 1 box of chocolates.

Stokes Seeds Ltd. (seeds)
P.O. Box 548
Buffalo, NY 14240-0548
(717) 695-6980
Fax Toll-Free 888-834-3334
www.stokeseeds.com
Free 112-page color catalogue; over 2,500
  varieties of seed.

Thompson & Morgan, Inc. (seeds)
P.O. Box 1308
Jackson, NJ 08527-0308
(732) 363-2225
Toll-Free 800-274-7333
Fax (732) 363-9356
www.thompson-morgan.com

Van Bourgondien Bros. (bulbs)
P.O. Box 1000
245 Farmingdale Road
Babylon, NY 11702-9004
Toll-Free 800-622-9997
www.dutchbulbs.com

In Canada

Alannah's African Violets
(pelargoniums)
Site 640, R.R. #1
Grand Forks, BC V0H 1H0
www.alannahs.com
Wide variety of geraniums.
On-line catalog.

Cruickshank's Inc.
780 Birchmount Road
Scarborough, ON M1K 5H4
Toll-Free 800-665-5605
Fax (416) 750-8522
Mail-order. Send $3 Cdn for 2-year catalogue
  subscription (6 issues).
Retail Location:
1015 Mt. Pleasant Road
Toronto, ON M4P 2M1

Dominion Seed House (plants, seeds)
P.O. Box 2500
Georgetown, ON L7G 5L6
(905) 873-3037
www.dominion-seed-house.com

Ferncliff Gardens (dahlias)
8394 McTaggart Street
Mission, BC V2V 6S6
(604) 826-2447
Fax (604) 826-4316

Gardenimport (bulbs, seeds, plants)
P.O. Box 760
Thornhill, ON L3T 4A5
(905) 731-1950
Toll-Free 800-339-8314
Fax (905) 881-3499
www.gardenimport.com
Send $5 for 2-year catalogue subscription
  (4 issues).

Hole's Greenhouses and Gardens Ltd.
  (plants)
101 Bellerose Drive
St. Albert, AB T8N 8N8
(780) 419-6800
Fax (780) 459-6042

Holt Geraniums (perlargoniums)
34465 Hallert Road
Abbotsford, BC V3G 1R4
Fax (604) 859-8308
www.holtgeraniums.com
Over 1000 unusual Pelargoniums.
  Send $3 for catalogue or search on-line.

Mason Hogue Gardens (plants)
3520 Durham Road #1
R.R. #4
Uxbridge, ON L9P 1R4
Send $2 for catalogue.

Seeds of Distinction (seeds)
P.O. Box 86, Station A
Etobicoke, ON M9C 4V2
(416) 255-3060
Fax Toll-Free 888-327-9193
www.seedsofdistinction.com
Catalogue by request only.

Stokes Seeds Ltd. (seeds)
Box 10
St. Catharines, ON L2R 6R6
(905) 688-4300
Fax Toll-Free 888-834-3334
www.stokeseeds.com
*Free 112 page color catalogue; over 2,500
varieties of seed.*

In England

Chiltern Seeds (seeds)
Bortree Stile, Ulverston
Cumbria LA12 7PB
England
(Country Code +44)
   229-581137 (24 hours)
Fax 229-584549
E-mail: chilternseeds@compuserve.com
Send $4 Cdn for catalogue

On the Internet only

www.garden.com
Gardenescape
710 West 6th Street
Austin, TX 78701
Toll-Free 800-466-8142
Fax Toll-Free 800-700-6604
Fax: (512) 472-6645
Internet site offering secure online ordering.

Growers/Distributors

The following list is an additional resource.
Contact these growers/distributors if you
wish to find a local retailer of some of the
plants discussed in this book.

Ball Seed Co. (distributor)
622 Town Road
P.O. Box 335
West Chicago, IL 60186-0335
(630) 231-3500
Toll-Free 800-879-BALL
Fax (630) 231-3605
Fax Toll-Free 800-234-0370
*Authorized wholesale distributor of Outback
Plants®.*

Dentoom's Greenhouses (spring cuttings
   and seedlings)
R. R. # 1
Red Deer, AB T4N 5E1
(403) 309-7700
Fax (403) 309-7701
*Member of the Proven Winners® marketing
co-operative.*

Four Star Greenhouses (grower)
1015 Indian Trails Road
Carleton, MI 48117
(734) 654-6420
Fax (734) 654-2795
www.fourstarpw.com
*Member of the Proven Winners® marketing
co-operative.*

Grimes Seed Co.
11335 Concord-Hambden Road
Concord, OH 44077
Toll-Free 800-241-7333
Fax (440) 352-1800
Authorized broker of Outback Plants®.

Harris Seeds
60 Saginaw Drive
P.O. Box 22960
Rochester, NY 14692-2960
(716) 442-0410
Toll-Free 800-514-4441 or 544-7938
Fax (716) 442-9386
www.harrisseeds.com
Mail-order nursery selling Proven Winners®.

Paul Ecke Ranch (grower)
P.O. Box 230488
Encinitas CA 92023-0488
(760) 753-1134
Fax (760) 944-4002
www.ecke.com
*Propagator of new hybrids in The Flower
Fields® line; distributor of Outback
Plants®, Sunscape™ daisy, Kientzler
New Guinea impatiens, and over 150
varieties of spring plants.*

Pleasant View Gardens Inc. (grower)
7316 Pleasant Street
London, NH 03301
(603) 435-8361
Fax (603) 435-6849
www.pvg.com
A Proven Winners® breeder.

Proven Winners®
426 West 2nd Street
Rochester, MI 48307-1904
(248) 652-1789
Fax (248) 652-4137
www.provenwinners.com
*A unique marketing co-operative which
develops new hybrid color varieties
distributed to select retailers in Canada
and the United States. Website includes a
search function to locate nurseries
authorized to sell Proven Winners® plants.
You can also phone or fax for this
information.*

Weidners' Gardens Inc.
695 Normandy Road
Encinitas, CA 92024
(760) 436-2194
Fax (760) 436-3681
www.weidners-gardens.com
*A founding member of the Proven Winners®
co-operative, this grower is open to the
public from April to September, and
November and December.*

Glossary

CALYX — the outermost protective layer of a flower bud, consisting of sepals, which are usually green and leaf-like, but in some plants (e.g., rhodochiton) are quite showy and can substitute for the petals

COROLLA — the petals that form the inner part of the flower, which may separate or fused into a bell or a tube (e.g., fuchsia)

CORM — an underground swollen stem that produces a new plant each year (e.g., gladiolus)

CULTIVAR — a variety of plant developed by a plant breeder by deliberately cross-pollinating two plants

HYBRID — a plant developed from cross-pollinating two plants with different genetic traits

LEAF AXIL — the upper angle between the leaf and the stem it grows from

NODE — the place on a stem (often slight swelling) where a leaf is attached and from which an axillary bud grows. New roots grow from a node on a cutting.

PICOTEE — a flower with a contrasting color around the outside edge

RACEME — an unbranched stem of flowers. Individual flowers are stalked and spirally arranged (e.g., hyancinth).

REFLEXED PETALS — petals bent backwards instead of flat or cupped

ROSETTE — a rose-like cluster of leaves or a group of leaves radiating from the same point on a short stem to give an effect like a green flower

RHIZOME — a swollen horizontal stem just below the soil's surface (e.g., canna)

SEPAL — an individual leaf of the calyx

SPORT — a part of a plant that is spontaneously different from the original. It may have variegated foliage or a different bloom. The sport can be removed and propogated. Many new varieties are produced this way.

STANDARDS — plants trained to a small, upright, tree-like shape: full standards are usually 4 feet (1.2 m) tall; half-standards are 18 to 24 inches (45 to 60 cm)

STOLON — a prostrate creeping stem, rooting at the nodes and giving rise to further stems and plants (e.g., strawberry)

TUBER — a swollen root used for food storage and reproduction e.g., begonia

Index